Indeed!

Life's Lessons Learned
in the
Darnedest Way

by

Dot Minzer

and her ever so wise collaborator

The Blessed Holy Spirit

CONTENTS

A Word About Emmaus

These essays were originally written as talks I gave to my Emmaus sisters at Sacred Heart Parish in Punta Gorda, Florida. My association with the Emmaus ministry began back in 2010 when I saw a little article in our church bulletin advertising an upcoming women's retreat. Retreat? Hmmm, I thought. It had been many years since I had been on a retreat. Maybe this was something I should do. I checked my calendar and it worked so I signed up. I wasn't prepared for what was to happen next.

The Emmaus Experience, I found, was very different from other retreats I had attended. This one was a retreat where women ministered to women. I heard fascinating stories and witnessed a love and sense of caring that resonated with me long after the weekend was over. I was soon to learn that the retreat, itself, was only the beginning. The best was yet to come in the way of monthly Saturday morning coffees where the ladies, who had experienced the retreat, gathered to keep its spirit alive. Here they shared their thoughts and insights, their friendship and their support. Here we all learned that none of us walk the Emmaus Road alone. What causes one to stumble and trip are the same boulders that others have tripped on, too. And in this sharing, a beautiful sisterhood formed. We quickly found that within each other we live the motto for which the Emmaus Ministry is known: Jesus Christ is Risen! He is Risen Indeed!

It was my Emmaus sisters who urged me to compile these essays into a book. I thank them for their persistence and their encouragement. In particular, I'd like to thank Laurie Druyor who relinquished her Saturday morning microphone so I could first share my stories; Dave and Marie Geggis and Dotti Vaivoda who painstakingly found all the errors my eyes had missed; Jane Ambrosino, my co-facilitator, critic, cheerleader and friend whose wise suggestions made this book better; and Kay Garris with her five dollar bill that supplied me with the "kick in the behind" I needed to get it done. I cannot fail to mention Ed, my dear husband and ever so patient sounding board, who with his simple thumbs up or thumbs down let me know if I was on the right track. Lastly, I must thank the best collaborator a writer could ever want, the Blessed Holy Spirit. His wisdom guided my every word. Indeed!

Prelude

I lost a very favorite cousin last year. Growing up we played with each other, fought with each other, took dares from each other, shared our most sacred secrets with each other. Just cousins, yes, but more like sisters in so many ways.

We were very different, Lois and I. Maybe that's why we got along so well. She was flamboyant, I was mousy. She was the actress, I the wimp. Playing Ethel Mertz to all of her Lucy Ricardo hair-brained schemes I willingly followed along. In so doing I shared in the glory when things went right, and more often than not, in the blame when they went wrong.

Once, when we were about ten, our grandma, putting away the groceries, opened a new bag of Pecan Sandies and gave us each one. Then she tucked the bag away in the cupboard above the sink saying we could have more later. That didn't sit right with Lois or with me. The minute Grandma left the kitchen, Lois put her finger to her lips and said, "Shhhh!" She went to the closet for the step ladder and easily retrieved the cookies which, without hesitation, we ate down to the very last crumb, polishing off the entire bag. I don't remember what Grandma said or did when she discovered the empty bag in the trash. But I do remember the stomachache I endured for the rest of that day which was punishment enough for my part in our "crime". In fact, until this day I cannot even look at a Pecan Sandie without feeling my stomach revolt.

So what does all of this have to do with the essays in this book? Just this: each one was written at a different time, some in a different place, with different ideas in mind. Each has thoughts to ponder and insights to share. However, if you read them all at once, you will suffer from insight overload, and your mind and your psyche might revolt. So treat this little book as you would a bag of Pecan Sandies. Read one essay at a time. Put the bag (the book) away between helpings and give yourself a chance to savor the taste of each essay on its own. You'll come away wanting more instead of hoping you never read a Dot Minzer tale again.

Motherhood and Wisdom

When Laurie, my Emmaus sister, first asked me if I would do one of our Saturday morning coffees I said, Hmmm! Let me think about it. First there was the question of the shoes. Even though I tower over Laurie in height, stepping into her shoes would be difficult. She would be a tough act to follow.

Then I had to take into account the window. You know, THAT window, the one that opens into one's soul. In my previous life, before retirement, I had given presentations of all sorts to many different groups of people; so speaking in front of a group wasn't a problem for me.

But the subject matter – religion, introspection, your spiritual life viewed through the prism of mine. Hmmm! I'd really have to think about that. And so I did. I thought. And I thought some more. And as usual, the Holy Spirit wouldn't leave me alone. You see, I am a writer, and although through Emmaus I have learned to walk with Jesus at my side, when it comes to doing anything creative, like writing a talk for all of you, it's the Holy Spirit who is and always has been – to use texting lexicon – my BFF, my best friend forever.

1

He knows when to encourage me, when to discourage me, when to stymie me, or when to inspire me, and when to just whack me on the back of the head to get me moving. And this is what he did this time. The conversation went something like this:

Me: "Ok, if I do this talk, what would I talk about? It's May. How about I do my talk on mothers?"

Holy Spirit: "Hmmm, maybe; but I think wisdom would be better. I vote for wisdom. After all, that's my signature calling card. And Pentecost, my special day, is right around the corner, you know."

Me: "Right. I hadn't thought of that. But wisdom? What do I say about wisdom? How about mothers AND wisdom?"

Holy Spirit: "Good idea."

Me: "But how do I. . ?"

Holy Spirit: "Don't worry about it. It'll be fine. I'll help. We'll do it together."

So motherhood AND wisdom it is. Here I am, the window of my soul about to be blown open wide. Just don't get caught in the whoosh as the fresh air comes rushing through. That will be the Holy Spirit, hanging around just to make sure I do this right.

Mothers. My mother, your mother, ourselves as mothers. What is it to be a mother? Surely the nine months a woman spends carrying a child in her womb is one good indication of motherhood. But I would suggest that that is only the smallest, tiniest part. In fact, sometimes it doesn't qualify a woman for motherhood at all. Instead, it is the years of caring and concern and nurturing and sacrificing. It's the years of lying awake at night worrying. It's the giving, guarding, guiding and cheerleading, the hand holding and even the letting go that comes afterward that qualifies one to be a mother. Maybe it's to your own children; maybe it isn't for children of your own. Maybe it is for nieces or nephews or, as a teacher, kids you had in school. Or maybe, as a health professional, patients you had at some time. Or maybe, as a business woman, someone you mentored. Or even the work you did itself, some life work you babied and nurtured, developed and raised to fruition. However our mothering skills developed or where, on whom, or to what they were applied, most women can claim membership in that Motherhood Club.

Motherhood, as I see it, has three parts. They overlap and interlace and sometimes it's hard to know when one part stops and the other starts, but still the parts are three.

The first is, for lack of a better title, "Motherhood in Training". That's when you are a child yourself and learning how to be a mother. You rock your dolly, boss your brother or sister around, and absorb all those motherhood traits by watching and listening.

Maybe with the monkeys motherhood is innate, but in the case of children? Well, as Dorothy Law Nolte writes in her beautiful poem of the same name, *Children Learn What They Live*. I paraphrase:

> If a child lives with encouragement,
> she learns to be confident.
>
> If a child lives with tolerance,
> she learns to be patient.
>
> If a child lives with praise,
> she learns to be appreciative.
>
> If a child lives with acceptance,
> she learns how to love.

My own mother wasn't a well-educated woman. She held no degrees in psychology or social work. She never even finished high school. Yet (and here it comes, Holy Spirit) I learned the wisest things I know from watching her. I learned things by what she did and by what she did not do. I learned things by what she said and by when she chose to say nothing at all. I learned when to stand up and when to stand back. Just as I acquired her recipes for German potato salad and Polish galumki by watching her make them, I acquired her recipes for motherhood by watching her live them.

My parents had very little money. We lived in rented apartments until I was grown. Just as I was ready to leave for college they finally acquired a small bungalow all their own. My mother loved that little house and set about to make it as special as she always dreamed her very own house would be.

She planted hydrangeas in the front yard, tomato plants in back. She painted a branch of dogwood blossoms on the living room wall and bought a new White sewing machine to make crisscross curtains for the kitchen. It is the curtains that I remember most. Done in white Dacron, each had ruffles etched in an embroidery stitch that her snazzy, new machine allowed her to do. She was so proud of those curtains and couldn't wait to show them off to me.

When I came home from school the next week-end she probed, "Well, what do you think?" She was looking for a compliment. She had been my praise giver for so many years and now she was looking for praise from me. But I was eighteen, full of "all about me" thoughts. "They're nice, Mom. Pretty." I was distracted. I had something going with my friends that night and all I was thinking about was getting ready. My shoes needed polishing so I brought the brown shoe polish to the kitchen to spiff them up. One dunk of the swabby applicator into the bottle and a quick yank pulling it out and – Oh my! There were brown shoe polish splatter dots all over one side of the new curtains. I stopped dead in my tracks as both my mother and I stared at the curtains in disbelief.

Even in the retelling of this story, something that happened over 50 years ago, I still get a sinking feeling in my stomach wishing that even now, all these years later, I could will that shoe polish back into its bottle and leave those curtains as beautiful, white, and unviolated as they were before I ruined them.

But it was what happened after the shoe polish splatter that I remember even more. My mother didn't say a thing. I'm sure every ounce of her being was screaming on the inside. But on the outside she took a step back, declared, "What's done is done," and concerned herself more with how bad I felt than anything else. I learned a very valuable lesson that day. Through her acceptance, I learned how to love.

So often, in dealing with my own children, thoughts of those curtains niggled in the back of my mind. Surely the tolerance my mother showed me enhanced my patience every time I mopped up milk from the dinner table. Surely it altered my reaction when footprints and cookie crumbs appeared all over my newly washed floor. Children DO learn what they live.

Motherhood. Part Two. Do you remember the first time you held a supple little newborn in your arms? Do you remember that awesome feeling when you realized you were responsible not only for that wiggly little body but for the sacredness of its soul as well? And as we raised our children, we thought ourselves so wise. Just think of the "wisdom" we had to impart to them:

"If everyone jumped off a cliff, would you jump too?"

"Close that door. Do you think we live in a barn?"

"Money doesn't grow on trees, you know."

"Don't make that face, or it'll freeze in that position."

"If you can't say something nice, don't say anything at all."

"If I talked to my mother like you talk to me...."

Can you hear yourself? Can you hear your mother? You didn't spend all those years "in training" for nothing!

Shortly after my first child was born, my mother came to see us. She gushed and praised and cooed just like a grandma is supposed to do. When the time came for Mom to go home, my husband and I took her to the airport. As we sat at the gate, waiting for her plane (You could do that in those days.), I fed my baby a bottle. When she finished I held her to me, encouraging her to burp. She obliged by spitting up all over my shoulder. "Yuck!" I said. "Now don't I smell just great?"

"You smell beautiful," my mother replied. "Don't you know?" she said. "Mommies are supposed to smell like that. You're wearing mommy perfume." After that, I never felt the same about spit up again. Mom looked at me with the biggest smile that day and said, "I am so proud of you. You are a wonderful mommy." And I beamed at her compliment.

The little baby I held in my arms that day is now 44 years old and a mommy in her own right. I still get a warm and fuzzy feeling when I remember what my mother said that day. It was her encouragement, just as Dorothy Law Nolte said, that gave me confidence and allowed me to be the person, the mother, I turned out to be. I compliment my daughter and her sister every chance I get, tell them how proud I am of them and what wonderful mothers they are. I hope that they, too, will have some warm and fuzzy feelings 20, 30, even 40 years from now from what I say to them today. As mothers we stumbled along, making mistakes as we went. It was literally "on the job" training. Sometimes we learned from those mistakes, sometimes we didn't. But we relied heavily on what we had learned watching and listening to our mothers.

That brings us to what I think might be the most difficult part of Motherhood, the letting go part. After years of being the director, of being in charge, of telling our children what to do and when to do it – the time comes when we must sit back and allow them the right to find their own paths, to make their own mistakes, to learn from those mistakes or not just as we did. And that is hard.

Some 15 years ago, when my younger daughter was the mother of two, small babies, her husband, an alcoholic, was in the hospital suffering tremors as the long abused alcohol withdrew from his system. As he screamed and cussed and yelled in the other room, the charge nurse came to the waiting room where I sat with my daughter and called out, "Mrs. O'Bryan?"

"Who is that?" I thought. I looked around. My little girl Annie and I were the only ones there. Surely she was looking for someone else. But no, she was calling my daughter to talk to her about what was happening. I sat there, in that waiting room, like a bump as my Annie, my precious little girl, my 25 year old daughter – the child I sheltered and protected and kept from harm for so many years – jumped up and went to the far side of the room to confer quietly with the nurse. It was not my place to be there. I was not part of the conversation. Every fiber of my being was crying out, "Talk to ME. I'm the mother here. I'm the one you should be talking to – not my little girl." But it was my little girl who was now a woman who talked to the nurse, who shouldered the burden of her very sick husband in the other room, who bore the responsibility of what was to come in the following days and weeks and years. That was a turning point for her husband, Chris. Today, he is 15 years sober and we are very proud of him. But that day, in that hospital, I had to drill myself to my seat to keep from taking over where I most certainly didn't belong.

Anna Quindlen, a feature writer for the New York Times, when turning 60, published her

10

memoirs. She titled her book, Lots of Candles, Plenty of Cake. After years of writing about motherhood she had some interesting insights into the role we all have played. Looking back on her years she pondered: what if, at 60, she could sit down with her 22-year-old self and have a heart to heart talk? What advice would she give herself? After much thought she realized that her 60 year-old-self could tell her 22-year-old-self nothing, simply because they did not speak the same language.

And that is, my Dear Holy Spirit, where wisdom comes into play. Your wisdom. The wisdom, that as we age, you give to us. It changes the way we speak. It changes the way we think. It changes the way we act. It gives us a language, an understanding, that we never could have had at age 22 – or 32 – or even 42.

There is no such thing as the wise, young owl, is there? No, it is always the wise, old owl. That's the way it is.

Socrates, that wise sage of yore, says, "True wisdom comes to each of us when we realize how little we understand about life, ourselves, and the world around us." In other words, when we were young, we thought we knew it all. Wisdom, which can come only with life experience, shows us how little we actually knew then, and if we are honest with ourselves, how little yet we even know now. But it makes us willing to accept it. And that is what makes us wise.

I will never forget the time, probably right around when I turned 60, that my husband and I were visiting our daughters who at the time both lived in Wisconsin. It was cold and icy. As we all walked from the car to the restaurant where we were going to have dinner, my younger daughter latched onto my arm so I would not slip on the ice. She had never done that before. Sons might be chivalrous; but daughters, at least mine, never were. But here she was, holding me steady on the ice. And I thought, this is what I used to do for my mother. Then I mused, are my girls starting to view me as old? As someone they need to look out for? What a weird feeling it was as I realized that, in some regards, the baton had been passed. It was just yesterday, or so it seemed, that I was the in the middle of what has come to be known as the sandwich generation, concerned for my parents on one side, my children on the other. Now, it was to be my daughters' turn in the middle, my grandchildren on one side, my husband and I on the other. And I guess the best thing for me to do is what wisdom counsels. Accept it. But that doesn't mean I will go down without fighting!

Wisdom also shows us how, over the years, we have become our mothers. We look like them. We sound like them. They have given us so much of themselves. When I look in the mirror and see my tummy that will never, no matter how much exercising I do, be flat, I realize that my mother's tummy was never flat, and so I say, "Thanks, Mother!"

When I see the hair on the side of my head that absolutely refuses to curl forward but only backward, no matter how much hair spray I use, I realize my mother's did the same, and I say, "Thanks, Mother!"

When I realize that the wisdom she imparted to me has become part and parcel of my life influencing me every single, solitary day I say, "Thank you, Mom. Thank you very much."

Oh, and the curtains? The ones splattered with shoe polish? For the next fifteen years that they hung in my mother's kitchen, the brown was carefully covered with white fingernail polish that made for bumpy spots all over the side. But it did hide my disaster and they served as a reminder of who I was and who I became all because of my mother.

Cocoon Catholic

Did you ever notice that when you ask someone what religion they are and they tell you they are Catholic – the term, Catholic, never seems to be enough? People will always throw a qualifier in there. They'll say, "I am a practicing Catholic," or "I am a fallen away Catholic." One might refer to themselves as a devout Catholic, or possibly say I'm born and raised Catholic. Once I had someone tell me they were a recovering Catholic. I'm not exactly sure what she meant by that; but, nevertheless, the word Catholic alone never seems to do it.

I suppose if I were to qualify my Catholicism, I might call myself a cocoon Catholic because, even as I grew physically in my mother's womb, through some mystical osmosis, her Catholic faith – ah, let's put a qualifier in there – her Polish Catholic faith grew inside me as well. Polish Catholic. That would be the correct way to identify my mother because her Catholicity was branded by her Polish roots. Hers was an open, loving, sentimental Catholicism, one that trusted more and worried less. Expectant mothers will hold their tummies and sing lullabies. When mine held me she hummed "My Chcemy Boga/We Need God," a Polish Catholic hymn. Mom's rosary beads, for she said the rosary every day, draped across her tummy and, as a result, across me as I grew within her and grabbed my being even before I was born.

Mom was sixth of seven children. When she was seven years old, her father fell on his way home from work at the steel mill, hit his head on a streetcar rail and died. The entire family, eight of them led by my grandmother, relied on faith, both emotionally and pragmatically, to get them through very difficult times. In the Polish neighborhoods of South Side Pittsburgh there was no organized St. Vincent de Paul food pantry; but if there was, my grandmother, with all her mouths to feed, might have been at their door.

And my father? Catholic, yes, but let's qualify his Catholicism, too. Dad was German Catholic. In sharp contrast to the softness of my mother's Polish Catholic faith, my father's German Catholicism was based on duty and obligation. Dad's was a scrupulous faith. He saw his God as an all-powerful being, where my mother saw hers as all-loving. While my mother did the trusting, she left the worrying to Dad.

My father was one of six children. Growing up on the north side of Pittsburgh, life was not easy for him either. He also lost his father when he was seven years old, his to the great influenza of 1918. The commonality of missing fathers probably, at first, had a hand in bringing my parents together.

Dad was literally raised in the church. His two uncles, my grandmother's brothers, were priests and, as their Holy Orders required, they looked after the spiritual welfare of their parishioners. However, they also cared for the temporal welfare of my grandma and her children. When my grandfather died, Grandma went to work as the rectory cook and housekeeper, first for Uncle Father Joe and later for Uncle Father Leo. All the children who were able, and that included my dad, worked as custodial staff for the parish plant. My father's day began at 6 a.m. with the ringing of the Angelus and ended when the last classroom in the parish school was cleaned to the nuns' satisfaction. While their faith emerged from different ethnic springs, both of my parents were immersed in Catholic life.

They were married in 1938. In Europe, at that time, Germany was busy dismantling the country of Poland. The Germans had no respect for the Poles, who – in turn – despised the Germans. The mutual hatred and mistrust that existed between the two countries in Europe bled into the United States as well. So when my very German father, Billy Schramm, brought his little Polish girlfriend, Rosalia Zawadzka, home and announced she would be his wife, it had to be their mutual Catholic faith that bridged the yawning ethnic chasm.

Take all the other qualifiers away; ours was a very Catholic home. I knelt on our hardwood floor each day to pray the rosary with my mother. I watched my dad usher at Sunday mass. I traveled with Mom to endless novenas and prayer services and watched my dad kneel by the side of his bed each night to say his evening prayers.

My entire life was entwined with the Catholic faith. Mom made sure that wherever we lived (and we lived six different places as I grew up, mostly apartment buildings) that we were very close, definitely within walking distance, to church.

Each place we lived was decorated "Catholic". There were statues, pictures, crosses, holy water fonts, and who knew what else in our home. This was my mother's touchy-feely, Polish Catholic faith. My father, the conservative German, loved my mother dearly and usually let her have her way. But in one particular apartment where we lived there was a long hallway off which the bedrooms could be found. Dad teased her that it would be a perfect spot for the Stations of the Cross.

My parents moved to East Cleveland, Ohio a few years after marrying and that is where I was both born and baptized. St. Philomena's Church became the hub around which my life would revolve. Mom, of course, volunteered herself – and later, when I was old enough, me – for everything. I sold raffle tickets for the church bazaar, worked the fish pond at the bazaar. I folded Sunday church bulletins on Saturday mornings, cleaned wax off the pews after Holy Week. I was a Sunday school aide, assisted the nuns with CCD, served coffee and cake to the visiting seminarians, did the dishes when they were gone, and I played the piano for entertainment at the Ladies Guild Potluck Dinners. Yes, my entire life revolved around church. I became (bear with me) a touchy-feely, scrupulous, ardent, devotional, prayerful, trusting, worrisome Catholic.

In the gospel of St. Luke we read:

"When He had seated Himself with them to eat, He took bread, pronounced the blessing, then broke the bread and began to distribute it to them. With that, their eyes were opened and they recognized Him; whereupon He vanished from their sight. They said to one another, "Were not our hearts burning inside us as He talked to us on the road and explained the Scriptures to us?" Luke 24: 30-31.

This breaking of the bread, blessing it, and distributing it to others is truly the sum and substance of the sacrament of Holy Eucharist. My faith may have developed with all those quirky qualifiers, but it did have a focus. As I grew up and grew old, it was the Eucharist that opened my eyes and burned in my heart. It was the Eucharist that came to truly define my Catholicism. Let me explain.

I was a precocious little person when I was young. An eager beaver, I was quick to learn and easily bored. The nuns did not know what to do with me. I finished my school work early and needed more to do. Sister Sheila, my second grade teacher, found a solution. She let me tutor my classmates.

That was the year we made our First Holy Communion. Before we could receive that holy sacrament of sacraments we first had to memorize the answers to the questions in the Baltimore Catechism. I knew them backward and forward right away. So Sister gave me her copy of the questions and placed me in the cloakroom to drill others. Over and over again, to one classmate and then another, I would ask, "Who made us?" And I would hear, "God made us." "Why did God make us?" "God made us to show forth His goodness and share with us the everlasting joy of heaven." Then I would ask, "What is a sacrament?" The answer: "A sacrament is an outward sign, instituted by God to give grace." To my very concrete seven-year-old mind, this created an amazing picture. I could literally see God, driving an oversized dump truck to church on the day of my First Communion to drop a ton of grace on me, grace that would obviously change my life and make me noticeably different.

It had been years since I had received Baptism, my first sacrament. And I certainly didn't remember it. But now, with Holy Communion right around the corner, I anxiously awaited the arrival of the truck.

When the big day came I had on my new white dress, my lacy veil. My mother did my hair in sausage curls and I was so excited. When it was my turn to approach the rail, I guess I was more taken by my new dress than by my new grace because I really didn't feel much different at all. I struggled with the host that attached itself to the roof of my mouth and worked my tongue to dislodge it. Sister Sheila told us to bow our heads and pray when we returned to our seats, which I did. I snuck a sideways peek at Cheryl Simon who was kneeling next to me. She snuck a peak back, and we both giggled. So much for the dump truck full of grace! Or so I thought.

What I didn't realize at the time, but have come to know so many years later – many years of growing up, getting my education, establishing my career, meeting my husband, raising my daughters – many years of receiving that Blessed Sacrament – the dump truck was there all along pouring grace upon me, showering me with help, guidance, direction, insight, and, once in a while, even wisdom every step of the way. Its cargo of Eucharistic grace spilled upon me and influenced every major decision and most minor decisions I have ever made.

My second grade vision was right all along. Eucharistic grace has made me noticeably different. It has been, and continues to be, the grace that shapes my life. I get out of bed each morning for daily mass because I know that truck is making another delivery, and I want to be there to get it.

Many years ago I decided to become a hospital Eucharistic minister. In essence, I became a truck driver for God, driving Him and His sacred cargo of grace to patients and shut-ins who, for one reason or another, could not come to church. This has influenced my life in ways that are not imaginable. So many people I minister to say, "Thank you," to me as I leave. My answer always is, "No, let me thank you!"

for it is I who is so privileged to be driving that truck of grace.

Hospitalization can bring anxious times. With concern over tests to be had, results to arrive, or important decisions to make, there is often a high level of stress in the hospital room. It is into this atmosphere that I poke my head in the door and say with a smile, "Hi, I'm from Sacred Heart Parish, and I have Holy Communion with me. Would you like to receive?"

"Yes." "Definitely!" "I've been waiting for you." These are some of the responses I get. We pray for a moment and when I give the Eucharist, I can see a tangible peace settle on the patient and the room. Sometimes there are tears. Sometimes my hand is kissed. The patient relaxes as he realizes he is not in his quandary alone. God is there too.

Then there are times I knock on the door of a hospital room, announce why I am there, and I'm greeted with, "Oh, I haven't been to church in years!" or "I'm not sure the church would still consider me Catholic" or "I haven't been to confession in a long time" or something like that. We are told, in situations like this, not to stand on rules or regulations. A hospitalized person is in a compromised state. No matter what their situation it

23

is appropriate to offer them the Lord. I respond with, "Well, I didn't ask you how long since you've been to church. What I asked was, 'I have Holy Communion with me. Would you like to receive?'" And this is where it gets interesting. I watch as someone who, possibly years ago, decided to go it alone and give up on God come to the realization that God never gave up on him. God was always there, just waiting to be recognized. After a pause and thoughtful deliberation I sometimes hear a very muted, "Yes, I would!"

This might sound funny, but at times like this you can almost see God smiling. I know I smile. He steps right up to take His rightful spot in the heart and soul of the person before me. Facial expressions change. A quiet ensues as I park my truck next to that patient's bed and God pulls the lever that opens the gate to spill His grace all over that person and inside him as well. Sometimes the person cries. Sometimes I cry with him. Always I am moved beyond words because I have experienced the very real presence of God.

Not too long ago I was visiting my daughter in Wisconsin. While attending mass at their parish church I noticed an ad in their Sunday bulletin. It was for the nearby Little Sisters of the Poor Assisted Living and Nursing Home. I said to my daughter after mass, "Not now, of course, but someday, should the need arise, that is where I want to be."

"Mom," she replied. "You are ridiculous. You've never even seen that place. How would you know that that is where you would want to be?"

I thought about my love of the Eucharist and replied, "Because, it says right there that they have daily mass and communion. That's all I'll want. That's all I'll need. That's good enough for me."

And it is, and will be, more than good enough for me. I wouldn't have to worry about the truck and its cargo of grace. It would make its delivery right to my door, every day. And what touchy-feely, scrupulous, ardent, devotional, prayerful, trusting, worrisome Catholic could ask for more than that.

Family

Growing up, my immediate family was pretty small. We numbered five. There was my mom, my dad, my older sister and me. My baby sister died when she was three years old; but we always included her in our count, because, well, she counted too.

Both my mother and my dad came from very large families. If you factor in all of them – and you really have to because we were all very close knit – the total came to 114 people. Grandmas, aunts, uncles, cousins, second cousins! There was always a herd of family around me.

I loved it. I loved the chaos. I loved the commotion. I loved the big parties. I loved holidays, going from house to house with someone related to me inside every one. I loved family, period. And this was always what I wanted for myself – a big family, a home with lots of kids, lots of uproar, lots of hugs and lots of love. I had my road all plotted out.

However, unbeknownst to me, God had other plans. He did provide me with a wonderful husband; but instead of blessing us with pregnancy after pregnancy, which was my plan, five years went by with nary a one. My first year of marriage was filled with hope, my second bolstered by patience. By year three and no babies I had become anxious and by year four I fought total frustration. So much for my plan and if God had His, it certainly was not one I could see.

We visited doctors but learned nothing. We subjected ourselves to medical procedures to no avail. We followed all of the doctors' suggestions, but got nowhere. This was, of course, the 60's and our options were limited. Medical science still had mountains to climb. So as we entered our fifth year of childless marriage, I finally gave up.

Giving up was not something I graciously did. Goal oriented, once I set my mind to something, big or small, I always found a way to get it done. But this? This was different. This was something over which I had absolutely no control. And I didn't like it.

My next step was based totally on female logic. I cried. I lay down on my bed one afternoon and bawled. I bawled and bawled. I worked myself up into a real frenzy. And do you know what? It actually felt good. It washed all my frustration away, all my disappointment, all my regret. My husband wasn't home so no one heard me but God and He just sat back and let me go at it. He patiently waited until I cried myself out.

When my sobs settled to sniffles, I sighed a very deep sigh; and that was when I felt the shove. God pushed me right over to the cupboard where I got out the phone book and looked up the number for Catholic Charities: Department for Adoption.

Oh, I guess that idea had sat in the back of my mind for some time. My husband and I had discussed it, but I always resisted. It was to be a last resort. To me it meant giving up. And as I said, it was not in my nature to give up.

But that day I did and God won. I could almost hear Him saying, "Well, what do you know. She finally got with the program." That was the day I let go of my plan and embraced His instead. When I hung up the phone, for the first time, I could see a road ahead of me. There was a path to follow.

Not that that path was easy. It was full of ups and downs and unexpected turns too. But it was a path. It wound through two long years of meetings, interviews, home inspections, autobiographical writings, providing friends for references –enough hoops to discourage all but the most serious. But most serious we were and our reward at the end of it all was our beautiful daughter, Elizabeth.

The baby announcement I wrote to send to everyone read:

A bit of news! Have you heard?
God sent us an angel on March 23rd.
Born February 7th she was but six weeks old.
And now she's ours to love and hold
And share our lives – which from now on
won't be the same –
Now that Elizabeth Gail came – to be ours.

And the same they never were. But that was only half of the happiness God had in store for us. Two-and-a-half years later, we were blessed with another baby. From filing out our application until our child arrived it was a total of only nine months. I phoned my husband at work the moment I received the call. He, who expected another long wait, said, "Son of a Gun! Son of a Gun!"

"No, Honey," I replied. "It's a girl. We have another daughter." I sent out a second announcement. This one read:

He must have liked the job that we did before
For He decided in His goodness to send us just
one more
Of His tiniest angels from up above
To share with us our lives and our love.
Ann Marie will be her name
And we are proud to be
The Daddy, Mommy, and Sister
of her adopted family.

Liz, our eldest, resembled her dad – if you consider each had two eyes, a nose, and a mouth. With a ruddier complexion and darker hair, stretch your imagination and she did look a tiny bit like him. On the other hand, Ann, our youngest – with red hair and freckles, looked amazingly like me. So many, many times when my daughters were young, the three of us would be out and about only to hear a perfect stranger remark how much this little girl looked like her mother. This was then followed by a quick nod to Liz and the comment, "You must look like your dad!"

"Yes, I do!" Liz would answer. Then the three of us would walk away chuckling. It was our secret that we were an adoption family. In some ways it made us special.

Having adopted children always brought questions from people. (It still does.) It is not that people were nosy. They were just curious. Everyone wanted to know, "Did your daughters always know they were adopted?" Yes, definitely. From the second they entered my arms I called them my adopted angels. They grew up knowing that "adopted" was a beautiful word. It was synonymous with love.

The second question which always followed was, "Did they want to know about their birth parents?" And I have to answer that, in our case – no, not really. I tried when my girls were teen-agers to tell them what I knew about their birth circumstances but they said they didn't care. I was their mom, and Dad was their dad, and that was all there was to it. Maybe their attitude about this came from what I said to them all the while they were growing up. I would say, "I don't understand it and you won't either; but somehow, some way, somewhere God planned us for each other. He decided that I would be your mother and you would be my girls. I'm so glad He did and I'm not about to question why." And I didn't. We didn't. And to this day, we don't.

While my husband and I were always very open with our girls about the fact that they were adopted, we never found it necessary to elaborate on that fact to others. In introducing them we would say, "These are our daughters, Liz and Ann!" The introduction was never punctuated with "These are our adopted daughters, Liz and Ann." That, we thought, would be silly. As a result, most people, with exception of relatives and close friends, had no idea that our girls were not our natural born children. This, too, presented some funny situations.

Once, when Ann was about 10 years old, she was playing down the street with some of the neighborhood kids. Suddenly she came running home and burst into the house in tears. "What's wrong?" I asked.

She answered, "They don't believe me. No one believes me. They say I am making it up so I can be important."

"What?" I questioned. "What are you making up?"

"That I'm adopted," she said. "I told them I'm adopted and they said I was lying. Even Christy's mom said I was lying and that I shouldn't make things up."

I hugged my daughter, told her not to be upset. I told her she was right and that the others just didn't understand and that I would straighten it out. And I did. I called Christy's mom to tell her, yes, Ann was adopted. She wasn't making anything up. A very embarrassed woman apologized to me, and later to Ann. She had no idea.

Thinking about that incident later I had to smile. Some kids might try to hide the fact that they are adopted, embarrassed by it, worried that others will think they are different. And here was my kid, proclaiming it to the neighborhood, proud of it, and in tears because no one believed her.

I know how we, my husband and I, feel about our daughters. We couldn't love them more if they did grow in my womb. But on our bedroom wall hangs a poem in a beautiful frame that lets us know how they feel about us. It was a gift to us one Christmas from our then college-aged Liz. Too broke to buy store bought gifts, she gave us this priceless present instead. The poem reads:

I may not have her eyes or her smile.
I may not have his height or his fingers and toes.
I don't have the same walk; I don't have the same nose.
I don't know where I came from, or how it came to be

That the parents I have were meant just for me.
Not born from their genes, I was born from their
hearts
And it's not hard to decipher, it was a pretty good
start.
God needed two people to shape and mold me right.
And they accepted the task with not one fight.
They knew it wouldn't be easy – I did resist a bit –
But they vowed that no matter what, they never
would quit.
And today . . .
I do have her morals, and her patience.
I do have his humor, and stubbornness, too.
I have their same values; I have their same views.
And, I know how I've become the person I've gotten to
be
From the people that were truly meant, just for me.
People aren't parents by just giving you genes.
Being parents requires a whole mess of things.
People become parents when they make you feel
whole.
People are parents when they give you your soul.

Not too long ago, as we were working on our
second glass of wine one evening, my husband and I
began to muse about our lives (as one will do on the
second glass of wine) recounting what was realized
and what was not, pondering the "what ifs" that have

passed us by. My husband surprised me by asking –
If, by some stroke of the wand, I was given the
opportunity to bear my own natural children, would I
have been willing to give up the two beautiful
daughters I did have the privilege to raise? And I
quickly, without hesitation, answered, no. Give up my
Liz? Give up my Ann? No, no way.

Both of our daughters are beautiful grown
women today. Each has blessed us with
grandchildren that are our joy. God took our
frustration and gave us two miracles. He knew
exactly what He was doing. For that we thank Him
every single day.

A while back I celebrated a milestone birthday
and everyone – my daughters, their husbands, and all
the grandkids – came to help me celebrate. For an
entire week it was chaos at our house – noisy, crazy,
beautiful, heavenly chaos. It was just the kind of
chaos I remembered from my youth. While we didn't
number 114, we did fill our house to the brim--with
family. And I realized I ended up exactly where I
wanted to be when I first got married. I came there by
one of God's less traveled roads, but I got there just
the same. I never did give up. I just gave in. I let go of
my way and lett God lead me through His.

Come as a Child

Over 2000 years ago John the Baptist said something very instructive. He said, "I am the voice of one crying in the wilderness. Make ready the way of the Lord. Make straight His paths." Wow, did you hear that? He said, "Make straight His paths." We were admonished way back then to make our paths straight. Well, I don't know about you, but somehow the paths I walk on my way to God are anything but straight. They twist this way and that way. There are hills to climb and sometimes some pretty low valleys. Sometimes my map is well marked and off I go only to have plans change quickly. I encounter road construction and potholes; I get waylaid by traffic jams. I look for road signs, but some of them get very confusing. How about you?

You know, though, our paths weren't always this discombobulated. When God first set them out for us they were pretty straight. It was we who added the detours; we who put in the right and left turns; we who made it necessary for our internal GPS to constantly recalculate.

No, our paths were pretty straight when we were first born. However, that was before we created our own agendas, before we put on our masks and adopted our maybes, before we built our walls and crafted our worries. Life was simpler then. Do you know why? I think it was because we trusted more and doubted less.

The Bible says, "Let the little children come to me. Do not hinder them, for the kingdom of God belongs to such as these." So let's talk a little bit about what it is like to follow the road to the kingdom – not as a baggage-laden, guilt-ridden, over-worried, fuss-budgety adult, but as a little child.

You only have to take a look at one of your grandchildren, a grandniece or nephew, or any other small child to see what it was like. Children are curious. The smallest of the small test everything. Touch everything. Shake everything. Put everything in their mouths to see what it tastes like. Now I am not suggesting that we put everything in our mouths, but you get the idea. When the littlest of our grandchildren come to visit what do we do? We put our expensive knickknacks out of reach because we know, without a doubt, that their little hands will be all over them. I remember once putting my grandson, then three years old, in his car seat in the back of our brand new car. Even I did not yet understand what all the buttons, knobs, and switches accomplished. It took him just two minutes to push every button, turn every knob, flip every switch, and re-adjust every air vent. If it moved, he moved it. It took me forever to put things back the way they were, all because of his limitless curiosity.

And then, children grow up. They turn into (gasp) adults. That insatiable desire to examine and investigate gets shoved aside. Grown-ups move inside themselves. They pretend. They worry people will know they don't already know it all so they feign knowledge and understanding. Sometimes they just remain content to know what they know and don't care to know more. The excitement of discovery goes away and gets replaced by humdrum. How sad!

Do you know what else little children are? They're honest. They don't calculate, parse words, or try to manipulate. They just say what is on their minds. If they like something, we know it. If they don't, we know that, too. Children call it exactly as they see it. Right is right. And wrong is wrong. Black is black, and white is white. The contingencies, the complexities, the "Yeah, but what about" mitigating factors – those grays, have yet to get in the way.

When a child gets hurt, what does he do? He brings that hurt to his mom or his dad. Maybe it's physical like a bruised knee or maybe it is just bruised feelings, but that hug from mom or dad makes it all better. Once that magic hug or magic kiss is given, tears quickly change to smiles.

Little ones don't hang on to hurts either. By the same token, they don't hang on to grudges. They haven't yet become embroiled in that adult miasma where hurts are left to fester, held close, and babied – some of them never to be let go.

I know a man who was hurt many years ago through what he thought was a caustic email. He told me he keeps that email on his computer to this day so he can go back, look at it, and seethe a little. He wants to be able to re-live that hurt whenever he wants. Pray tell, why?

Little children are something else, too. They're trusting. When I was little, my family often went for picnics to the nearby metropolitan park. Sometime during the day, and as often as my sister and I could coax him, my father would walk us over to the swings and push us high, high, higher than the tree tops. I remember the thrill of flying so high, trying to touch the leaves on the trees with my toes. Then, just as he had us soaring as high as the swing could go, he'd push hard one last time and come running through under the swing and end up standing in front of us with a big smile on his face listening to us squeal with delight. I had complete trust in my father when he did that. I held on tight and said, "Harder, Daddy. Push harder. Push higher! Higher!", because I knew that I was safe as long as he was there. Trust? Uh huh! You find it in children.

Years ago I went to a group dynamic building workshop that the school district I worked for sponsored. They thought that if we could learn to trust our colleagues, we would cooperate more, share more, and that the school environment would strengthen, which in turn would produce better teaching and better learning by our students. (The wisdom of the 80's!) Anyway, one of the exercises the facilitator had us do was the "Fall Backward and Trust Me". In teams of three, one person had to agree to a backward free fall while the other two stood behind to catch her before she reached the ground. When it was my turn to fall, it took a fair amount of convincing for me to do it. Eventually I did it but I didn't like it. A little kid, on the other hand, would think it fun. He would say "Geronimo!" and just let go. Of course someone would catch him! That's trust.

This trust thing is the child-like quality that I, as an adult, have the most trouble with. I think I remain curious – at least to a socially acceptable degree. I judge myself truthful and I am better than I once was at keeping my big mouth shut when it needs to be shut. I am comfortable outside of myself, at least most of the time. But it is the trust thing that bugs me the most. No matter how often I hear the adage, "Let go; let God!" I find it so hard to do. I have spent more nights than I care to remember lying awake worried about something. I like my worries. I need them; I nurture them, baby them. My husband, who worries about nothing, snores away each night while I lie awake deliberating which worry to tackle next.

This same sage man, my husband, upon waking up, has said to me, "Dot, do you know why you worry?" And I ready myself for his philosophical explanation.

"No, dear," I answer. "Why do I worry?"

"Because you want control. You think that if you worry enough you can manipulate things and make them turn out the way you want them to." And. you know, he's right. I think that if I pray long enough and hard enough, and if I lie awake enough nights with determined thoughts in my head that things will turn out the way I want. I'm a worrier, yes; but I'm really a wannabe manipulator and control freak in disguise. When I think about it that way I realize my worries are just plain silly. Why can't I, just as I did as a child, fly as high as I can, let my toes touch the trees,

and trust God will come running through to face me
with a great big smile on His face because He knows I
have placed my trust in Him?

There is another expression of trust little
children display. You see it at picnics or amusement
parks at the end of a long, busy day when they fall
sound asleep in the arms of their mom or dad. They
play as hard as they can all day long. They go, go, go
until they get so tired they just – fall asleep –
wherever they are. One minute they can be eating an
ice cream cone and the next they are sound asleep.
No worries. Just trust – trust that their parents will
keep them safe, get them home, and get them tucked
into bed. Not a care in the world as long as they are in
their parents' arms.

Joan Walsh Anglund wrote a beautiful poem
about childhood. It says

"The work of the water is bubbles!

Day is the job of the sun.

Green is the business of gardens.

And the duty of children is fun."

Do you think when God, our Father, said His
kingdom belongs to those who would come as little

children, that this is what He meant? He wants us to have fun, to live curious lives, to grow outside ourselves, and to limitlessly enjoy this beautiful world He created for us. He wants us to play hard and worry less. Then, when we get tired, He wants us to rest in His arms; and when it is time, to just fall asleep and understand that He is there to take care of everything. He is there to get us safely home.

A Self-Professed Project Junkie

You know, when we walk the Emmaus Road we often encounter obstacles. It is not an easy path. There are bumps in it. There are ups and downs, twists and turns. Although we might think that those obstacles we encounter on our journey are unique to us, when we meet fellow travelers, we quickly realize that our obstacles are not unique at all. We quickly learn that we have all tripped over that same boulder, lost our bearings at the same turn. We are not alone in our clumsiness, and in spite of our best efforts, we sometimes lose our way. Let me share with you a couple of the pesky boulders that continue to trip me. Maybe you have come across them, too.

First, some background. I am a self-professed project junkie. I thrive on being wrapped up in one project after another. If there was such a thing as a support group for people like me, you would find me standing up and saying, "Hello, my name is Dot, and I am a projectaholic!"

So what do I actually mean by a project? By "project" I mean any endeavor – short term or long – that consumes my time, my mind, and sometimes, my entire life. What makes me a projectaholic is that I somehow find a way to do many different projects all at the same time. I might complain and gripe, moan and groan about all that I have to do. However, if you took all those projects away from me, just like any other addict, I would suffer from withdrawal.

There was a point in my life, before I retired, that I managed to hold down a full time job (Project 1), pursue an advanced degree (Project 2), rear two children (Projects 3 and 4), be a Girl Scout leader (Project 5), teach CCD (Project 6), put dinner on the table every night (Project 7), clean my own house (That's an iffy 8.), knit Christmas presents for the family, (Project 9) and still (Project 10) keep a smile on my husband's face. In those days I couldn't be sure if I was in charge of my life or my life was in charge of me.

I didn't pick up all those projects at once. I was like a juggler who tossed first one plate in the air, then two, then three – until all ten plates whirled about my head, the entire menagerie in motion.

If even one of them lost its orbit for a nanosecond, all of the plates could come crashing down. Somehow, though, they didn't – which just reinforced my daring, boosted my confidence. "I can do this!" I said to myself as I continued on – a self-professed, self-reliant, project junkie.

When I retired, I swore off project junkiness –
not unlike any addict who finally decides enough is
enough. This time, I told myself, things would be
different. We moved to a different state and made all
new friends. No one had to know about my
"addiction". I would spend my retired years on my
fanny doing the writing and the reading I always
dreamed I would have time for. I would not raise my
hand to volunteer for anything.

I remember one sunny afternoon, shortly after
we settled in. I was comfortably settled in the lounge
chair on the lanai next to a glass of iced tea. My
husband came out, looked at me sitting there, smiled
and said, "That's nice!"

"What's nice?" I asked.

"You," he said, "doing nothing." I have to
admit. In my determination to swear off my
"projectaholism", even I was smiling.

However, as any true addict will attest, it isn't
easy to follow through. Good intentions are easily set
aside. Soon the laid back laziness of the lanai lost its
glow, and my fingers started to drum. Da-drum! Da
drum! Da drum! I needed more to make me happy.
And that is when I took my hand out from under my
fanny and began to raise it once more. I heard myself

say, "Sure, I can do that." "Uh huh, no problem, I can help you out." "I'd be happy to!" Before long I found myself, once again, in that familiar plate whirl, trying to keep all my "projects" in balance.

Does all of this sound familiar? See, I know I am not alone in my project junkie-ness. Many of you are in it, too.

I come by my addiction honestly. I inherited it from my mother. She was the Queen. Mom didn't drive, but that didn't stop her. She walked – to church, to work, to clubs (where she always served as an officer), to pot lucks, to choir practice, to the fabric store so she could make curtains, bedspreads, altar cloths for church, clothes for me, aprons, and even ring pillows for each of her twenty-seven nieces and nephews as they got married. I watched her whirlwind spin about me every single day; and although I never consciously said, "I'm going to grow up to be just like that," I did.

There is an upside to being a Project Junkie. I accomplish a lot. Sometimes I actually amaze myself with all that I can do. There also are, however, the downsides; and herein lie the boulders on my Emmaus Road.

First there's the matter of patience. I have none – at least I have none innately. Patience is in direct conflict with my Project Junkie gene. I'm used to getting in there and getting things done. It's very hard for me to have patience with others that don't.

That doesn't mean it's impossible for someone like me to acquire patience. Over the years I have worked very, very hard to do just that. But I have to admit, when I go to a Penance Service at Christmas or Easter, and the priest asks me to identify one area of my life that is wanting, my lack of patience always tops the list.

Being a Project Junkie I also tend to be very independent. Now that can be a good thing. It can also turn into my trip-you-up boulder #2. You see, I seldom ask anyone for help. I don't know how to do it. I am uncomfortable when help is offered. More than likely I will turn help down.

Just last week, I came home from the Emmaus Retreat, with a full blown head cold. When one of my good friends learned that I was sick she called to tell me she had made a casserole for me and would bring it over the next day. I said to her, "That isn't necessary. It's very nice of you, but it's really not necessary." I said this in between coughs and sneezes.

This friend knows me well. She knows how I am so she replied, "Well, Dot, you better say yes to it, my dear, because if you don't, I am going to have to throw it away. I made it just for you!"

Oops! As I picked myself up after tripping on that boulder I realized I was looking square at the other side of the help story. It is so easy for me to do for others. I can do for ten others with one hand tied behind my back and never miss a beat. However, to allow others to help me? That, for me, is hard.

Sometimes people are forced into letting others help them. My mother was one of them. After spending over 60 years doing for everyone else, she contracted the very debilitating disease of rheumatoid arthritis. Wheelchair bound, she had no choice but to sit by while others did for her. For someone such as her – and me – and so many of you – asking for help or accepting help is very hard. We are used to juggling all of our plates by ourselves.

When the crippling arthritis finally hastened my mother's death, Father Al, our assistant pastor and a good family friend, eulogized her at the funeral mass. I remember his words so well. He said, "Rose spent her entire life doing things for others. But nothing, not the swelling in her joints, not the crippling in her hands, not all the pain she endured, nothing was as difficult for her as these last few years when she had to graciously allow others do things for her."

Boulder #3 for me is sort of a combination of #1 and #2. When I trip on this one, though, quite often it is my poor husband, Ed, who ends up with the skinned knee. We both share in chores around the house, but even he will admit the scales tip in his favor. I do the lion's share because – well, same old story, it's just easier for me to get in there and get things done. I go my merry way picking up this task and that and then, all of a sudden, I'll start to feel – overwhelmed. Unappreciated? Put upon? You know what I mean. My nose gets out of joint. Then I'll blurt out, "Do I have to do everything myself? Can't I get some help here?"

Just about then my totally oblivious husband, unaware that he has just become the target of my poor-me pout, looks up from the magazine he is reading and says, "Well, why don't you ask? I'm not a mind reader, ya' know."

And he's right. My Boulder #3 is not that I don't ask for help. It's not that I refuse help. It's that I grumble and complain about the help I don't get that I really feel I should get even though I'll never ask for it and would probably turn it down if it were offered. Go figure!

The term Project Junkie is my own. But there is other nomenclature to describe people like me. Have you ever heard of the Type A personality? You might remember those tests that determined personality types. They were really big back in the 60's and 70's. I Googled them to see if they were still around. They are. They're alive and well and they are officially named the Myers/Briggs Personality Assessment. For the modest fee of $59 you can take them online and determine your personality type.

Here's how they described a Type A: an individual who is ambitious, rigidly organized, sensitive, impatient, one who takes on more than they can handle, one who wants other people to get to the point, someone who is proactive. I don't need to take the test. I know. That's me.

Then there's the Type B. People with a Type B personality generally live at a lower stress level. They are steady workers, enjoy achievement but do not become stressed when they do not achieve.

I am reminded of something that happened some years ago that put these two personalities into play. Let me share. My daughter, Liz, was 15 years old at the time and the proud possessor of a driver's learning permit. It was a cold, January day and we were headed to the mall, Liz at the wheel. We took the back roads where I thought it would be safer. All of a sudden the car hit a patch of ice and we were off on an uncontrollable slide to the side of the road, surely – I thought – to land in the ditch beside it. In the five seconds or so that came next I quickly listed our options in my head:

1. Ed is out of town. We are on our own.

2. We aren't going fast enough to be seriously hurt.

3. We do have our seatbelts on so we won't be tossed.

4. We just passed a house. I can go there for help.

As my Type A personality was plotting out our survival plan, my daughter – a definite Type B – was busy with her own reaction to our plight. When we finally came to a stop, inches before the ditch, she said to me, "Mom, I'm so sorry."

I regained my composure then said, "It wasn't your fault, honey. It was the ice. You couldn't help it."

"No," she said, "Not because of the car. I'm sorry for what I said."

"I didn't hear you. What did you say?" I asked.

"I said, OH SH----!"

I could only laugh. Then she laughed. It relieved us of our tension; and I said to her, "If ever there was an appropriate time to use that word, this was it!"

Looking back at that incident I realized it was a case study between the A and the B, between the Project Junkie and the non-Project Junkie. It was reflected in the two ways we handled that impending crisis: me with my mental list of what we would do, how we would get out of it, organizing things even before they happened, just in case they did happen --- and Liz with her laid-back acceptance, punctuated by her spontaneous profanity. The case can be made that I was the mom and she the kid and that made the difference. Now, however, twenty-eight years later, she is still more likely to take a "wait and see" attitude over things while I am more inclined to take charge. As Myers Briggs states (and this is how they make money on their research) the conflict between these two personalities in the workplace, and even in our personal lives, makes getting along challenging. It also makes for interesting mother - daughter exchanges; but that is another topic for another time.

Well, that's it for some of my boulders along the Emmaus Road. I'll bet you have tripped on them, too. I continue to work on my patience and will for some time to come. It's nice to know that when I do fall flat on my face, one or several of my Emmaus sisters, my sisters in Christ, are there to help pick me up – if only I remember to ask. I promise I'll try.

The Rosary

October, the month of the Holy Rosary! I thought I might, this month, talk a little bit about the rosary. It's fitting that the full name for this devotion is "The Mysteries of the Rosary," because that little string of beads upon which one says this prayer has, indeed, mysteriously wormed its way into my life.

I'd like to say that I have said the rosary every day of my life. But I haven't. While I say it quite often now, years went by when I didn't say it much at all.

My mother did say the rosary every day. The beads she used came woven among her wedding flowers, and over the years she used them so often she actually wore them out. She fingered the crystal beads to the point that they slid back and forth on the rosary chain. Unless you counted out ten, it was difficult to know where the Hail Marys left off and an Our Father began – unless you were my mother, who could have identified each and every individual bead by touch. She continued to use that rosary, and only that rosary, until she died. Then she took it with her to her grave.

I'd like to share with you some of my rosary memories. They are warm memories, nostalgic to be sure. If you were raised in the church or even if you weren't, you may have rosary memories, too.

Memory Number One:
Move Over Bill Haley and Silence Those Comets!

As I was growing up I did say the rosary every day – along with my mother – on my knees – on the hard wooden boards of our dining room floor. Why the dining room? Because that was where our Stromberg Carlson combination radio/phonograph was located. And for the rosary, we needed the radio.

Station WERE was the number one listened-to station in Cleveland, where both Ed and I grew up. For Ed, six years older than me, WERE was where he found cruising music played by the station's number one disk jockey, Phil McLean. He and his buddies, hair slicked back, would cruise the drive-ins with the top down in his '57 Ford, Bill Haley and the Comets blasting from the car radio.

McLean had a signature sign-off. Every night, at exactly 7:45 p.m., you could hear him say, "In the meantime and in between time, have a ball, won't y'all?" Just like that, at 7:45, the rock'n'roll music would end, and in its place you'd hear Shubert's Ave Maria. A soft baritone voice would proclaim, "Direct from downtown Cleveland, St. John's Cathedral, we bring you – the rosary." My dear husband, a convert later in life, had no appreciation back then for Shubert or the baritone or the rosary. In Phil McLean's "in between time" he said he and his buddies were not having a ball – at all. Their groans, he told me, could be heard throughout the drive-in.

But for me, 7:45 was an entirely different story. This was my nightly routine – dinner, bath, pajamas, and Hurry! Hurry up! It's going to start! Shubert, the baritone, and then – the rosary. I'd be with beads in hand, on my knees, on that floor, right beside the Stromberg Carlson and my mother.

Memory Number Two:
The Amazing Road Trip

One day, Mom announced an amazing road trip. We would, she said, travel to the cathedral and say the rosary there IN PERSON. I was so excited. I was going to be on the radio. We got all dressed up (for the radio!) and right after supper took the bus downtown. We got off on Euclid Avenue and walked three blocks down 9th Street to the cathedral. St. John's was a massive church, cool, dark, and at that hour of the evening, pretty quiet except for a dozen or so souls gathered in the Mary Chapel. I looked at my watch. It was just a few minutes to broadcast time. We took our places in the pew as a priest walked in, knelt before the statue of Mary, flipped some switches, and began --- "In the name of the Father, and of the Son, and of the Holy Ghost."

It was really no different than any other rosary I had ever said and yet it was very different. I'm not sure I even really prayed that night. I was so enthralled with who might be listening (besides God and Mary, that is). If anyone else WAS listening, did they recognize MY voice? That night, we were rosary celebrities, rosary stars. I wonder if my husband (whom I would not even meet until at least ten years later) was groaning that night. I'd like to think he was not.

Memory Number Three:
Count the Cows then Count the Beads

My dad got two precious weeks of vacation every summer, and every year our family made the most of them. We traveled north to Canada, south to Florida, east to New York, west to the Mississippi and every place between. Dad had wanderlust, and vacation time was the only time he got to indulge it. Every time our family took a road trip my mother kept my sister and me busy. We had our own maps to follow the road. We had drawing pads to make pictures. We played road games like Highway Bingo and Hangman. Then we counted cows.

When the games were done, we brought out our rosaries and we prayed together. We each took turns leading a decade. We prayed for each other and for safe travels, giving thanks that we were lucky enough to be on this road trip at all.

Memory Number Four:
You're Already on Your Knees, so Why Not?

When I was in grade school, we didn't have lockers like kids have today. Instead we had a cloakroom in back that ran the width of the room. It was sort of like a long hallway where we hung our coats, hats, boots, gym shoes, school bags, and everything else we lugged to school. I remember that cloakroom as being hot, stuffy, and smelly with all those things inside. This was the early 1950's when, along with the fire drill, we also had the air raid drill. At the sound of that warning siren the nuns herded us, not outside as they did for the fire drill, but back into the cloakroom. They told us to kneel facing the coats, bend over, and cover our heads with our arms – which was difficult to do because our heads were already submerged in our coats. We had to stay there for a prescribed length of time. So what better way to keep us quiet and in place while on our knees than a few decades of the rosary? The Hail Marys came muffled, but none the less, I'm sure they still made their way to heaven.

Memories. Recollections of the way things used to be. But what about today? Today we live in a very different world. While there are still many who make the rosary part of their daily prayers and there are still families that say the rosary together, many more identify the words "Hail Mary" with a football pass. While many carry a rosary in their pocket or purse, many others wear it around their neck like jewelry or let it hang from their car's rear view mirror for bling. When someone says they are going to have a Come-to-Jesus-Meeting, it doesn't mean he plans to spend time with God.

Kids in Cleveland, like everywhere else, still do cruise around in cars; but the rap or rock music they listen to will not be interrupted by the rosary. So then I just had to know. If not the rosary, what was broadcast each evening at 7:45 on that station of my youth? Thanks to the Internet I was able to learn. WERE is now a Talk Radio station. Proselytizers of every political point of view can be heard each night, expounding on their own individual creeds. You might even, on certain nights, be able to catch a reverend or two. (I noticed Rev. Al Sharpton's name in the line-up.) But God will most likely not be the topic of conversation. There will be no Shubert, maybe a baritone, but definitely, no rosary. Yes, things do change.

I heard someone criticize the saying of the rosary once. They said, "Why do you say the same thing over and over again? Hail Mary! Hail Mary! Hail Mary! It's tiresome."

Really? Then I quoted the best response I ever heard to an opinion like that. I said, "Do you ever tire of hearing your husband, or your mother, or your child say, 'I love you?' No, you enjoy hearing it over and over again. Well, each Hail Mary is an 'I love you' to the Mother of God. She never tires of hearing it either."

I do carry my rosary with me wherever I go. It is as important to have with me, I feel, as is my driver's license or a credit card in my wallet. I never know when I might need it. Not too long ago I was passing through a security checkpoint on a visit to a museum. All bags had to be searched. "Any metal?" asked the guard as he rummaged through my purse.

"Just my rosary," I replied as he opened an inside pocket.

A big smile came across his face and he said, "A rosary's just fine. No dangerous weapon there."

I thought about how special the rosary was to me, how I have turned to it in times of need, how I clutched it as my mother, when she was dying, clutched hers; how it has given me a connection to both Mary and her Son. No weapon? All in your point of view, I thought as I passed through the checkpoint. All in your point of view.

Being a Turkey

When I began writing this talk I thought I had the perfect idea. It was November. I would write about the different ways you can say thank you: hugs and tears, letters and presents, giving advice – and taking it too; all ways one can express gratitude to someone else.

As I sat before my computer screen, my very blank computer screen, it remained just that, blank. None of my ideas found a home. Rats! Apparently, I thought, my writing buddy, the Holy Spirit, did not like my choice of topic. So I asked Him, "Ok, it's November. It's Thanksgiving. What else, if not giving thanks, do you want me to write about? And quietly, I heard him whisper – *turkeys*.

Turkeys? Turkeys. I have to admit, it made me smile. Turkeys. Hmm! A stretch of faith to be sure, not to mention a stretch of the imagination. But then I started really thinking about it. Turkeys. Well, maybe. It might just work. Before you knew it, the keyboard began to click; and little by little, the computer screen began to fill. The result? My talk for you this morning – on turkeys.

Turkeys, as you well know, were a main source of food for our early Pilgrims when the winters were cold and crops not yet planted. Benjamin Franklin was so inspired by their contribution to the first settlers he wanted to name the turkey our national bird. He was voted down, of course, and the eagle was chosen instead. Thank goodness! Because today, in our vernacular, it's a great thing to soar like an eagle or to be eagle-eyed. However, if someone calls you a turkey, well that's an entirely different story. A turkey might look grand with his stately girth, his fanned out feathers, and his pompous way of walking; but walking is really all he can do. In fact, the domesticated turkey weighs so much that even if he wanted to fly he couldn't get his body off the ground.

It's also rumored that turkeys are not particularly bright. It's said that if it starts to rain, the turkey farmer wants to get his birds into the birdhouse as soon as possible because, if they are left in the barnyard during a rainstorm, they will stare at the sky and gawk at the rain. With their mouths open wide they'll keep looking up while the rain rolls right down their throats until they drown. True? I'm not sure. It just might be turkey folklore; but it does point out quite clearly what people think of the mental quotient of a turkey. To be called a turkey today is, well, certainly not very flattering. When people do dumb things or say something lame or insensitive, we call them turkeys. And those are the turkeys I write about today.

We've all been there. We have all been turkeys at one time or another. One of my classic turkey-isms actually occurred on Thanksgiving Day itself. I had 30 people coming for dinner and with dishes to cook, tables to set, chairs to gather, spots to get off the wine glasses – to say I was distracted that day was an understatement. One of the turkeys that day, the one designated to be eaten, was in the oven while the other turkey, me, decided it was time to check on the first one's progress. So, potholder in left hand, I opened the oven door then proceeded to reach in with my right hand to check. "Yeow!" I screamed as I burned my hand. That was stupid, I thought, nursing my red and blistering fingers. Then, what did I do next? I switched the potholder from left hand to right then proceeded to reach in with my left hand and burn it as well. Dumb? You bet. The "from the oven" turkey was delicious that day but the other turkey ate it with two sore hands.

Sometimes when we behave like turkeys, as in the case of my Thanksgiving Day debacle, we hurt only ourselves. I was the only one that day who ate dinner with blistered fingers, and others enjoyed a laugh at my expense. There are other times, however, when our being a turkey hurts others. Quite often it involves, like the real turkey that stands in the yard looking up and drowning in the rain, one's inability to keep one's mouth shut.

My sister, two years older than I, had a difficult life. Suffering from epilepsy and the side effects of medication she took to control it, she was often shunned as a child, left out of childhood games and friendships, and denied many of the opportunities I had and on which I thrived. Her gains were minimal compared to mine, and when she did find success, my parents praised her immensely. One such success was a part-time job she held while in high school. She worked in the boy's clothing section of a downtown department store. We were all, including me, very proud of her.

She saved her paychecks for Christmas. Under the tree she had beautifully wrapped presents for us all. Mine was a sweater, a pink, purple, and cream-colored sweater with three-quarter-length sleeves that were the fashion at that time. My sister was very anxious for me to open my gift. She looked at me with anticipation as I took the sweater from its box. I held it up and instead of oohing and ahhing as I should have done, I said, "Purple? Why did you buy me purple? Pink? I don't even like those colors." Well, my mother's look shut me up, but the damage was done. My sister was crushed. Put down and embarrassed, she was effectively shunned one more time, this time by her thoughtless turkey of a sister. I tried to walk back my words that day, but once out of my mouth there was no way I could stuff them back in.

In time that sweater, with its pinks and purples, became one of my favorites. The more I wore it, the more I liked it. As my sister saw this, I am sure in some way it made up for my blather on Christmas Day. She never mentioned the incident to me again. All these years later I still find myself thinking about it – especially when I wear something pink or purple, colors I have learned to love. That day, my very big mouth certainly earned me the title of Christmas Turkey.

Why is it we open our mouths and hurt others? Do we have to prove something to ourselves? Do we have to prove that we are better, smarter, more clever than others? If so, it is just to ourselves that proof is given because I am sure on that day when I ridiculed my sister's present, my parents thought I was none of the above.

I want to tell you a story about my father. I adored him, not because he was one of those larger-than-life dads, because he wasn't. No, my father was a timid man; quiet, sensitive; and when I look back, I realize he was insecure in many ways. When Dad married my mom, he found more than a wife. He found a safe, supportive niche within our family where he thrived.

Dad loved to tell my sister and me stories, stories about his childhood, memories of his dad, his brothers and sisters. You could tell he enjoyed his stories much more than any of his listeners. His eyes lit up as he told them. One favorite tale involved meeting his youngest sister at a trolley car tunnel after the trolley had broken down. He came to the rescue, got her out of the dark tunnel, and returned her safely home. It's not that the tale is important, but the fact that he loved to tell it; to re-live the events in his own mind of a time when he was the hero.

On each of the many times we drove by that trolley tunnel it was like flipping a switch. He'd start again with the story. My sister and I would look at each other, roll our eyes, and say to ourselves, "Here it comes again." Then, one inauspicious afternoon I decided to be bold. "Dad," I said, "you tell us that story every time we pass this tunnel. We're getting tired of it. When are you going to stop?"

"I'm sorry," he said. "I didn't realize I was boring you." Then, after that, he did – stop. He never mentioned this memory of the trolley tunnel again. As I said, my dad was a timid man. While I credited him with many reasons to crow, to his own way of thinking he had very few. As hero of the trolley tunnel he had a reason to be proud. Now I had taken it away. Turkey? Yep, I think so. It made me enough of a turkey that when I re-live my memory of the time I destroyed his, it is humbling.

We often make turkeys of ourselves, don't we? And our mouths and the words that come out of them are often the cause. When our husbands do nice things for us like running the vacuum or washing the dishes do we say, "Gee, thanks, honey!"? Or do we say, "You missed a spot."

When we talk with our kids, do we question their decisions and criticize their choices, certain as we are that they cannot possibly exist without our advice? Or do we keep our ever-so-wise opinions to ourselves and only be there for support?

When we learn a great bit of gossip, does it burn a hole in our verbal pocket until we can tell someone else? Or can we recognize it for what it is, set it aside, and not repeat it?

Do we insincerely patronize people when we are with them, then turn around and hypocritically judge them when they leave? All of those things make us "turkeys" not only on Thanksgiving, but all through the year.

When you come right down to it, it's an ego thing. We like to feel important. When we look up at ourselves, with our noses in the air, it also means we are looking down – down our noses at others. And to think we've been blaming all this turkey stuff on our mouths so far! Heavens to Betsy! Maybe we should be blaming the nose!

This is exactly why, I am sure, the Holy Spirit wanted me to talk about turkeys. A picture comes to mind right now of that pompous, oversized bird, strutting across the farmyard. It's raining and, you know, he'd be just fine and he'd never drown – even if he kept his mouth open – if he just kept his nose out of the air.

So, if we blame our noses instead of our mouths, think of all the great and wonderful things our mouths and the words that come out of them can do. They can praise. They can compliment. They can encourage. They can forgive. They can instruct. They can inspire. They can embolden. They can give thanks. They can love.

My father had another memory. Thank God it was one I didn't spoil. When he was a young boy, the family lived in McKees Rocks, Pennsylvania near St. Mary's Catholic Church where my Great Uncle Leo was pastor. Dad and his older sister, my Aunt Tresa, did the custodian's work around the parish grounds. One of the things they did each day, three times a day, was ring the Angeles. He just loved to tell us this story.

A few years ago I wrote a poem about his memory. It was a poem of love for my dad. I think, in some way, it was my mea culpa for the trolley tunnel memory I ruined. Dad died over thirty years ago so I could never share it with him. But maybe, as he sits up there in heaven, keeping an eye on me, he listens. If so, indulge me as I share some words of love for him right now.

"Did I ever tell you," he'd begin,
and I knew, of course, he had.
But I'd look his way and shake my head.
"No, I don't think so, Dad."

With dreamy grin he'd settle in
with a tale he loved to tell,
I wanted to remember it,
so I needed to know it well.

"The Angelus. It was our job.
We rang the start of day.
Tresa, ten, and me, I was eight.
Still, we trudged and made our way.

"Up those steep and narrow stairs
we'd soar.
Our feet?
They barely touched the floor.

"I can still hear her yell,
my hand tight in her grip,
 'Be careful. Hold on.
Watch out. Don't slip.'

"Six o'clock.
So quiet, so still.
And it stayed that way
- - - up until - - -

"We grabbed the line, and it grabbed us back,
a rhythm quickly found.

It swung us high and the bells began
their piercing, certain sound.

"Jump high! Reach down!
Three. Times three. Times three.
'Come! Pray!' the bells would say.
'Come share our litany.'

"The angel of the Lord declared,
'Hail Mary, full of grace.
Behold the handmaid of the Lord.'
How the wind whipped past my face!

"'Be it done to me as is your word,"
the Virgin Mary replied.
'And the word was made flesh,' answered the
wind,
gusting from every side.

"Oh how we shivered! Oh how we froze
as we tugged with all our heart.
Our eyes were with tears when finally we came
to what was my favorite part.

"An explosion of ringing, on and on,
singing matins to God on high!
My arms now tired, I watched the sun
begin its ascent in the sky.

"Then, all at once, it was quiet again.
The glorious bells were done.
We made our descent of the steeple steps
one, by one, by one."

Quiet now, Dad sat and stared,
still in that other day.
But then he smiled and I could see him
tuck the memory away.

He'd keep it safe
till sometime when
He'd need to tell it
once again.

Tell it again, Dad, share it anew.
I need to know it well.
Someday your grandchildren will want to know
and I'll be the one who will tell.

There, Dad. That was for you. And I'm sorry I was such a turkey.

Words of love. Words of encouragement. Words of compliment. Words of praise. We need to use them more often. We need to be cognizant of all the words that flow from our mouths because they are like feathers from a torn pillow, or maybe a plucked turkey. Once released it is impossible to get them back. They fly in the air. They stick to your clothing. They take on lives of their own.

Let's hope those feathers are words to make us proud, not ones that we later regret. Let the turkeys we know be the ones served <u>on</u> the table – not only on Thanksgiving Day but all the year through – and not those <u>at</u> the table instead.

Noses and Roller Coasters

I want to talk about two things this time. Noses and roller coasters. What could they possibly have in common, you ask? Well, wait and see.

I've spoken about my Polish mother many times before. I've talked about her love and her devotion to her Catholic faith. I've talked about her wisdom, her kindness, and understanding. However, I've never told you about her sense of humor. She, along with her Polish sisters, always kept us in laughter. Each had a ready stash of jokes to share. If a joke was "G" rated it would be told in English. Then my sister, I, and all of our cousins, would get to giggle along. If it was a joke of a more mature variety, the language would quickly switch to Polish, and our younger generation would be left in the dust. One particularly silly joke I remember had to do with the comedian Jimmy Durante, nicknamed "The Schnoz" because his nose was so large. My mother asked, "Do you know why Jimmy Durante has such a big nose?"

"No," I replied. "Why?"

"Well," my mother explained. "When God was handing out noses, Jimmy was hiding behind the door to heaven. He misunderstood and thought God was handing out roses. 'Roses!' Jimmy exclaimed. 'I love roses. Give me a big one.' And so, God did."

Which brings me to the first thing I want to talk about today – noses – in particular – big ones. Lots of people have big noses today – not necessarily the flesh and blood kind of nose that's found ON our face but rather the other kind of nose, the nosey nose, the one that is found IN everyone else's face. The kind that is happiest when it is in everyone else's lives and business.

It's not really our fault, we say. It's the way the world is. The world we live in encourages us to know everything about everybody and everybody else to know everything about us. Such is our 21st century world of social media. Just think about it. There's email, Instant Messaging, listserves, texting, Facebook, Face Time, Twitter, You Tube, Skype – each one an avenue of access other people's lives, and should we choose to allow it, other people's access to ours. A virtual panacea for the overactive, nosey nose! To make it even easier on that nose, one can access all of those avenues from a small, tiny, compact, carry-it-in-your-pocket smartphone that will gladly alert you when there is something new your nose must know.

I don't take part in those social media outlets. I don't Tweet and, while I have many friends, they are of the flesh and blood variety that I meet for lunch or invite to my home for dinner. I "like" a lot of things but don't feel the need to expound on my "likes" to the world.

There are many upsides to my desire to abstain from social media. My daughters, who are 21st century warriors, do not understand – yet. To their dismay they ask, "Why not, Mom? If you had a Facebook Page, you could keep in touch with everyone. If you followed Twitter you would always know what was going on." The question then arises. Do I need to always know what is going on? And is it necessary for me to keep in touch with everyone? As far as I am concerned, the answer to both is a resounding NO! I have tons of relatives and many friends. If I kept in touch with all of them all of the time, I would go crazy.

My daughters, both happily married, are mothers of young children. They and their husbands are building careers in the middle of an awkward economy. Life, as expected, does not always run smoothly. Do I always need to know what is going on in their lives? Absolutely not. Always knowing what is going on is like being on a roller coaster ride at the amusement park sitting in the seat beside them. You can always count on it to be a white knuckle ride.

I'll bet you thought I would never get to my second topic – roller coasters. Personally, I hate them. When my kids were little, I took them to the Great America Amusement Park near our home in suburban Chicago. It was chock full of coasters that were, in my opinion, instruments of torture. There was the American Eagle, the classic wooden variety; the Batman that let you ride upside down and backward at the same time; the Demon that did the loop-de-loop; the Ragin' Cajun that spun 360 degrees through hairpin turns; the Viper that let you experience what it's like to be inside a cyclone. (Now I ask you, who would be nuts enough to put themselves willingly inside a cyclone?) You name it, Great America had it, and my kids wanted to ride them all. Those were years of torment.

Then, finally, the day came that they were old enough to ride those monsters on their own. I eagerly dropped them at the gate and let them ride all by themselves. I'd find a good spot from which to watch then wait for the ride to start. I would shout to cheer them on as their car left the platform. I'd give them thumbs up when they passed me by. I'd wave to them whenever the car appeared round the curve, and then

I'd rush over to the exit gate to meet them as they got off. They loved a hug when the ride was over. If their faces were flushed pink and they were laughing, they relished a high five. If they came down the ramp white as a sheet filled with relief, I'd commiserate instead. That's what good mothers did.

So now, here we are, all these many years later. My daughters are not riding as many real roller coasters any more, but they do ride more than their share of proverbial ones. And by always knowing what is going on in their lives, you're asking me to get back into the coaster car and ride with them again. No, thank you. If I did, this is what would happen. When their coaster would climb, I would climb too. I'd sit on pins and needles anticipating what would come next. Should their car plunge, so would I. Every one of their ups and downs in life would take my stomach along with them. When their car careened around an unexpected bend I would emotionally toss from side to side. My daughters, much younger than I, would absorb the throws and pitches. But my old body? It would get battered around. When the ride was over, the crisis past, more often than not, my daughters would leave smiling while I dragged my beat-up behind off the exit ramp. That's what happens when I ride the ride along with them. That's what happens when I always know what is going on.

It's so much better when I apply the same tactics I did when they were young. My grown kids appreciate the thumbs up. They love the high fives. They are grateful for the hugs, the smiles, and for the commiseration too. What they really want, and need, is to ride their ride on their own; and my nose needs to let them.

Wise me! I talk as though that is a very easy thing to do, let them ride on their own. It's not. It wasn't back all those years ago at Great America, and it isn't today.

Keeping one's nose out of where it doesn't belong can be very difficult. And this isn't just with our children, but with all those "others" we love, too. I have a sister whose ride is the cyclone, proverbial albeit, but cyclone just the same. When I call her each week I always hold my breath when I ask, "What's new?" There is always some full-blown crisis underway or else one smoldering on the horizon. It might be financial, it might be medical, it might be social, but there's always one. Her cyclone can get to spinning so fast that it appears, to me, to be out of control. That's when "I-know-better" me sticks my nose in and tries to help. After a while we tame her tempest, and things settle down. Whew! I think. That was close. And then, just when I think we are in the clear, she finds a way to get things spinning again. I've come, over the years, to realize that her cyclone never will stop. The funny thing is, her equilibrium inside her storm is not affected. She is used to the ride. When I join in, get into the seat beside her on her ride, I'm the only one who ends up getting dizzy. I'm the only one to toss my cookies at the ride's end.

Sometimes my children or even my sister ask me to join in on their ride. Sometimes they need me at their side. When that happens, I gladly get into the seat, even though I know what will happen to me. However, should I invite myself in? Bad move. They look around, see me there, and guess what? That's when my nose, where it doesn't really belong, puts their noses out of joint.

I'm put in mind of a silly little hoopoe bird my father brought home once when I was a little girl. Dad always brought home unusual things – things that tickled his fancy and that he thought would tickle ours. Such was this red plastic bird. It was about twelve inches long, six inches high, with a round body supported between two pencil thin legs. Its thin neck matched the legs and was connected to another ball that served as a head. It had a yellow plastic beak and goofy feathers on both the top of his head and sticking out his behind for a tail. The body and legs were joined in such a way as to form a fulcrum for what became a little teeter totter. If you placed the bird in front of a dish of water, the body – between the legs – would swing back and forth, the beak seemingly drawn to the water. Eventually the head would wobble its way down to the dish, the nose would get wet, and the bird would appear to take a drink. Once it "drank" its fill and the nose got wet, it would bounce back upright again until the nose dried out. Then it would wobble its way back to the water. I don't know how this happened, probably some obscure physics principle, but it did bring a smile to our faces, and that is what my father had in mind when he brought it home.

Thinking about that bird, I wonder, is he me? I put my nose into my children's lives, into my sister's life. No, I shouldn't do this, I say, so I quickly back away. Then I think maybe I should help or could help. So I put that nose back in again. Nope, not a good idea, I decide. So, just as quickly, I pull it out once more. Should I? Shouldn't I? Should I? Shouldn't I? It's so hard to know.

I have a seven year old grandson who comes up with the most off the wall things. The other day he was having a philosophical discussion with his father, my son-in-law. He told his dad that he liked to eat shrimp. His dad said, "Gee, Brock, I didn't know you liked shrimp."

"There's a lot you don't know about me, Dad," he replied. I said that my daughters did not yet understand the upsides of not knowing everything. They will one day. That day will come when their children are grown and have switched from the real roller coaster rides to the proverbial kind. That is when young Brock's prophetic answer, "There's a lot you don't know about me, Dad!" will pay its dividends. It should be that way. We are better off when our nosey nose stays out of places it does not belong. It keeps others from getting their noses out of joint. In many ways, that's also how everyone wins – by a nose.

Note: By way of explanation this talk was given at a Day of Reflection for Emmaus sisters from the many different parishes in our diocese. Our theme for that day was "We Are All One Body".

Feet

Those of you who have heard me talk before know that when I sit down to write it is my very best friend and writing partner, the Holy Spirit, who sits down with me. Like best friends, there are times when He can be agreeable and reassuring, and other times when He can be downright incorrigible. Let me show you what I mean. Our conversation about this talk went something like this:

Me: Ok, The theme I'm supposed to follow for today is "We Are All One Body". I'll write about how we are all alike, what we share, what we have in common. Then I'll add how we are different, each bringing his or her own uniqueness to the whole. What do you think?

Holy Spirit: What do I think? Bor-ing.

Me: Boring, huh? Ok, how about how we all need each other, how we are there for each other, supporting each other?"

Holy Spirit: Maybe, but I have a better idea.

Now I want to tell you that, in my experience, the Holy Spirit's "better ideas" are usually off the wall. So guardedly I said, "Just what exactly do you have in mind?"

And that's when I heard Him say, (Honest, He almost giggled when He said it), "Feet. I think you should write about feet."

"Feet?" I said. "Why feet?"

"Well, they ARE a part of the body, aren't they?" He had me there.

"But that's not exactly what we had in mind," I said, "when we said body. We didn't mean THE body."

"Why not? You've got to admit if you talk about feet it won't be boring."

He had a point there. However, the Holy Spirit always does have a point, doesn't He? The more I thought about it, the more I thought Ok, I give up. Let's give it a whirl. So I put some big girl shoes on my feet and buckled down to write about your feet, our feet. After all, we are one body. We have to start somewhere. So why not start at the bottom . . . with our feet?

Over the years I have been more than unkind to my feet. I have tried to squeeze them into some ridiculously awkward places – into high heels with ultra-pointy toes that in no way resembled the shape my feet were supposed to be; into mukluk snow boots – the kind lined in so much fluff and fur that your feet sweated so badly the only possible outcome could be toe rot. Yep, I have done some pretty nasty things to my feet over the years. In fact, I have even been known to put a foot or two – in my mouth.

God loved feet. In fact feet are mentioned three hundred and three times in the Bible. Twenty-seven separate times it talks about washing or taking good care of one's feet. Remember what happened at the home of the Pharisee? In Luke, Chapter 7, Verse 44, Jesus says, "I entered into thy house, Simon, and thou gavest me no water for my feet; but she (Jesus is referring to a prostitute) with tears hath washed my feet, and with her hairs hath wiped them." Christ, Himself, washed the feet of His apostles the night before He died. In John, Chapter 13, Verses 13-14, Jesus says, "If I, being your Lord and Master, have washed your feet, you also ought to wash one another's feet." It all means God had a lot more love for feet than I have ever shown for mine.

Feet! I don't know about you, but every time I see a newborn baby I look at her hair, or lack of it. Then I look at her eyelashes. Next I see if her tiny hand will grip my little finger. Then, lastly, I unwrap her blanket so I can see her feet. Do you do that? I always want to see her feet and hold one of those tiny things in my hand. I don't know why. Maybe I, too, realize that feet are important. You know, throughout life, the mind might make all the decisions, but it is the feet that carry them out.

When I was a little girl, my mother always called me the "I'm Gonna Kid." She'd say, "Did you make your bed yet?", and I'd say, "I'm gonna." Did you pick up all your toys?" "I'm gonna." It was always "I'm gonna." You see, my mind really hadn't made itself up yet to do those chores my mother expected of me, so my feet never got moving to get them done.

Today, as an adult, I have to admit that when it comes to house chores my mind can still get stuck in the "I'm gonna" mode. With tasks I make up my mind to do, though, I can become rather fleet of foot. It is the feet, without a doubt, that carry us forward. It is the feet that make all the difference.

Now, since this is a day of reflection, let's take a minute to do just that – reflect on where our feet have taken us, the roads we have traveled, the smoothly paved variety and the muddy quagmires that bogged us down, the trudge and drudge we've had to endure; and, on the plus side, the dancing those feet have allowed us to do. We want to keep moving forward, though, so let's do a little Michael Jackson moonwalk as we move forward and travel backward at the same time. Ok? Here we go!

Every life, every road, comes chock full of decision points: what to study in high school, whether or not to go to college, what job to take, whom to marry, where to live, how to raise our kids. It goes on and on, and each decision we make shapes our life as it unfolds.

Dr. Seuss makes this point in his ever so popular poem, *O The Places You'll Go*. He says:

> *"You have brains in your head.*
> *You have feet in your shoes*
> *You can steer yourself*
> *Any direction you choose."*

That little poem is true, up to a point. We do call the shots. Attitude, Perseverance, Fortitude, Determination – all those buzz words you find on those posters in forward thinking office buildings. They do play a large role. They do propel us on our road in life. However, sometimes the road itself that we travel is one not entirely of our own choosing. Sometimes something outside of us puts a road beneath our feet.

Let me tell you a little story about by husband, Ed. When he was a boy he didn't dream of being a policeman or a fireman. No, he watched the men with their hard hats climb the utility pole in his backyard and dreamed of working for the telephone company. He could climb those spiky foot holds, wear that clever leather belt with all those neat tools attached, hang suspended at the top of the pole, and fix all that needed fixing. A little boy's dream, huh? So when he graduated from high school he put that dream into motion. Ohio Bell hired him right away. He came home from his interview on cloud nine; his whole life, as he saw it, plotted out in front of him. College? Well, there was no money for that so why even bother.

Then he had to take a physical, and somehow someone saw something in his back that they thought might cause a problem with pole climbing and he was unhired as quickly as he was first hired. No longer was that road he had all plotted out there. Now what?

He had to make another choice, turn, find another road in another direction, with different stops, different turns, different people walking on it. That was scary!

Ed had taken some drafting classes in high school so a neighbor down the street offered to get him a job in the engineering department of the company where he worked, polishing off and finishing up little details on the drawings the engineers had developed. Well, not what he wanted, but it was a job. He'd work in an office! Where he had to wear a long sleeved dress shirt! And a necktie! Yuck! He dragged his feet – or maybe it was his feet that dragged him – off to work. Actually, once he began, he found he enjoyed this job very much. He was learning a lot. More than that, he enjoyed the engineers he worked with. He had never spent much time in the company of college educated men. Next thing you knew they were convincing him to save his money – for college – a road he wouldn't have even considered before. Once his mind was made up, it was those feet again that carried him off to Ohio State University where he majored in Mechanical Engineering.

When he finished his studies he returned to those same encouraging engineers but, this time, on an entirely different footing. Many more doors were open to him, many more opportunities from which he could choose.

It was then that one of those engineers invited him to a party where he met this pretty young girl, me. He spent the rest of his life not climbing poles, but walking – and much of the time dancing – along with his wife, me, down his road, my road, our road – the one we shared together.

Ed and I are very blessed. We have good health and sufficient money to enjoy our retirement. We'll be married 50 years this summer and we thank God every day that pole climbing was not his future. We know others who are not as fortunate.

I had a good friend, Dawn. She and I, years ago, were both communion ministers at our church. In fact, Dawn and her husband were both active members at St. Francis. They spent most of their Saturdays at soccer games, involved in the lives of their three beautiful sons. One day Dawn's husband came home from work and said to her, "Dawn, you are my best friend, you are my soul mate. I could never hope for a better friend than you." And then he said, "But I have met someone, someone who has given me a kind of feeling that I never felt before. You must understand, Dawn. I can't let this chance go by." With that, he asked her for a divorce. He left her to fall through what she thought was the most secure, sure-footed road there ever was. Yet now, here it was disintegrating beneath her feet.

My cousin, Dick, walked an amazing road. When he left the army back in the 50's, he began selling insurance policies door to door. He had the right attitude. He exhibited fortitude, perseverance, determination, all those poster board goodies, and because of them, in the years that followed, he got one promotion after another. It took him from policy peddler in Cleveland to the number two man at one of the largest, most prestigious insurance companies in the world. A limo driver was now driving him every day from his impressive home in Connecticut to his glass walled high rise office in New York City. He was the epitome of the American dream.

Today he suffers from Alzheimer's, and someday his wife will help him tie his shoes as he won't remember how to put them on his feet. Both he and his wife hold on as tight, as the road they walk roils beneath them.

Then there is my friend, Ginny. Her husband got out of bed one night to get a drink of water. He stumbled in the bathroom, fell, had a heart attack and died. No sickness, no illness. Death. Just like that. How does one find one's footing after things like these happen? How does one regain his or her path?

So many of us have struggled with things like that. Disease, divorce, death, brick walls all, crumbling paths that abruptly disappear. Life changers, things that make feet freeze in place so they cannot move forward at all. Road signs taken away, all one can cling to are mights and maybes. Suddenly, without warning, the "I will's", the "I want to's", even the "I'm gonna's" are replaced by "What now?" or "Where do I go from here?"

Years ago I took a trip out west. This was when the GPS was but a twinkle in some scientist's eye. I got one of those AAA Triptiks to help. It was a little spiral bound booklet with flip pages that showed me step by step the way from my home in Cleveland to San Francisco, California, and back. You know what I mean? They still have them, I think. Anyway, I had planned my trip carefully, knew which stops I wanted to make along the way, knew which sights I wanted to see. And the Triptik had it all plotted out with precision – ideal for someone like me who is and always has been directionly challenged.

However, that isn't how it works with life, is it? Sometimes life is like someone ripping pages right out of the middle of your Triptik leaving you stranded somewhere in the midst of the Painted Desert as you try to find your way back to Cleveland. It is true. Life **is** what happens while you are busy making plans.

Sometimes God asks us to carry burdens as we walk our road, crosses to bear we call them. Sometimes they can be pretty heavy. And if you should happen to encounter a muddy patch while you carry your heavy load, well, your feet can sink pretty far into that mud and moving forward once again becomes very difficult.

Let me tell you about my daughter, Liz. Her husband was without a job during much of the recent recession. Times were tough for them for quite a while. She told me how, at one time, she prayed they wouldn't come in the night and repossess her car as she was two months behind on her car payment. Thwup! That was one foot stuck solidly in the mud. In the middle of all this, she gave birth to a little boy who was hydrocephalic. He needed a great deal of medical care and specialized therapy, all requiring resources and insurance that Liz and her husband simply did not have. Thwup! Foot two stuck as well. What does one do when one becomes mired in the mud? Well, I'll tell you what they did. They settled for payment plans. They cut their budget to the core. They kept plucking one foot after the other out of that muck until finally – and it took years – they reached solid ground. Both Liz and her husband are gainfully employed today; their bills are paid, and their son, my grandson, Brock, is a feisty, thriving little boy. Their struggles, at least for now, are behind them. Certainly there will be other muddy patches in their road. They'll have other crosses to carry; but they'll be just fine. A poem I spotted tacked to her refrigerator door the last time I visited them tells me this is so. It reads:

Don't Quit

"When things go wrong as they sometimes will,
When the road you're trudging seems all uphill,
When the funds are low and the debts are high,
When you want to smile but you have to sigh,
When care is pressing you down a bit,
Rest if you must but don't you quit!
Success is failure turned inside out,
The silver tint of the clouds of doubt.
And you never can tell how close you are.
It may be near when it seems so far.
So stick to the fight when you're hardest hit.
It's when things seem worse that you must not quit."

Edgar A. Guest

A few years back we bought our first car to have a navigation system. What an improvement over that old Triptik! I was both thrilled and amazed at all it could do. The first time I plugged in an address and asked it to take me there I discovered that I could choose any one of three different routes to get to my destination. Then I also discovered that I could ask it to avoid or allow freeway travel, ferry crossings, toll roads, restricted roads – in other words I could custom tailor my travel as well. Wouldn't it be nice if we could custom tailor our travel down the road of life? Just picture it! Avoid all potholes. Check! Avoid all muddy patches. Check! Avoid uncertainties and brick walls. Check! Allow clearly marked road signs. Check! Allow smooth sailing throughout all of life. Check!

Hmmmm! That's not to be. So let me leave you with one last little story about a man who was totally dissatisfied with his lot in life. He did not like the road God chose for him to travel, and he did not like the cross he was asked to bear. And so he complained to God.

"God," he said. "I just can't travel this road or handle this cross You have given me to carry one day longer. It is just too much. I know we must all bear our burdens in life for that is what life is about. But please, God, could I have another – a different road; or if not that, at least a different cross that might be easier for me to carry?

God wisely and generously replied, "Certainly, my son. Come into the room of crosses with me. We'll see what we can do. Place your cross here and we will take a look around to see which other one you might wish to carry."

The man was elated. He removed his cross from his shoulders and placed it on the floor. Then he began to make his way around the room. He paused at each cross he encountered. No, he thought, not that one. Hmmm! No, I certainly could not endure that. That one is much too heavy, and I could never hold its weight. No. No. Each cross he encountered he quickly rejected until at last he came to one last cross all by itself in the corner. "This one," the man said. "I think I can handle this one." He picked the cross up and settled it upon his shoulders. It felt just about right. "Yes, this one," he said to God. "I'll take this one."

"But, my son," said God. "That is your cross, the one you put down when you first entered the room."

There is a moral to this story. Whatever cross God gives us to carry, whatever challenges come our way, He also gives us what we need to shoulder them. He never leaves us alone with our burdens but stands right beside us to help us tote our load. Whether we encounter brick walls, watch our road disappear, trudge through mud, or dance our way through – even though we might not recognize Him, God is there.

Just like the father that lets his little girl or boy stand upon his feet and hug tight his waist so they can dance around the room together, God says, "Here, stand upon My feet. I'll guide your feet where they need to go. You won't stumble. You won't fall. Just keep your arms about Me and your feet upon Mine and you'll be fine. You can count on it.

Ears

There was no argument this time. When the Holy Spirit suggested that we write about ears I was in total agreement. After all, we had talked about our big mouths and how they get us into trouble. We had written about noses and how we struggle to keep them from where they don't belong. We had done a piece about feet and the places they take us if we only just put one in front of the other. So it was just logical that ears would come into play at some time or another and this was as good a time as any.

Once that was decided, I settled down to write. However, no ideas would come. Try as I might, I hit a brick wall every time. So I went back to the Holy Spirit and said, "Ok, this was Your idea, too. I could use a little help here. How am I going to attack this?" And just like that, it was like a switch was turned on. Everywhere I went I saw or heard something that had to do with ears. Long ago memories from my childhood started cropping up in dreams. Passages from scripture at morning mass contained references to listening to God's word – thoughts about ears everywhere! TV commercials, music playing on the radio, articles in the paper! It actually became eerie. Every time I encountered one of these little gems I quickly jotted it down on a notepad I keep in my kitchen drawer. After a while, I said, "Ok. Ok. Enough already! I can do it now. I'll take it from here." What follows is the result: Ears by Dot Minzer and her ever so wonderful partner-in-writing, the Blessed Holy Spirit.

Ears. They are good for many things. The glasses that sit upon my face would have a hard time staying in place were it not for my ears. Pray tell, where else would I lodge all the many different pairs of earrings in my jewelry drawer if not on my ears? I realize my 17 year old grandson might suggest my nose, but thank you, grandson, especially for me, that would be quite a stretch. Kidding aside, we surely all agree our ability to hear is what gives our ears their value. God knew this too. In the Bible, He exhorts us to hear His word over eight hundred times.

However, I'd like to suggest something else. While hearing is the standard meat and potatoes job of our ears, I think the most significant thing they can do is listen. Same thing you say? Just semantics? No, not really. As a matter of fact, hearing and listening are two very different things, and often they can get in the way of each other. I'll show you what I mean. First let's talk about hearing.

Our world is full of sound. Some of it comes at us from the outside. Some of it consumes us from within. Some of it is beautiful. Yet, a lot of it is just, well, noise. However, there's a funny thing about that noise. We have become so accustomed to hearing it and living with it that, if taken away, we are lost without it. I know people, maybe you are one of them, who turn their T.V. on first thing in the morning and turn it off last thing at night. I know other people who keep it on even at night because the noise coming from it is part and parcel of their very psyche. I imagine they might suffer withdrawal if it were taken away.

Noise. Think about all the things in your house that beep, play music, buzz. Your dishwasher? Your microwave? Your washer? Your dryer? Your refrigerator? Your oven? Everything comes with its own built in notification system to keep you in control of your ever so busy, multi-tasking life. Then, on top of that, there is that modern little blessing – the smartphone. Not long ago I broke down and bought one. When I first brought it home, the thing made all kinds of noise. If I got a phone call, it rang; if I missed a call, it beeped. If someone sent me a text message, it clinked; and if a voicemail message came through, it clunked. I was told that if I had a Facebook account (which I don't) and one of my "friends" posted something new, another sound (I don't know, maybe a "twang" would occur.) If someone I knew, or didn't even know, chose to tweet something on Twitter? You guessed it, the phone would sound again. One day, shortly after I brought the phone home, it literally sat on my kitchen counter with a life of its own, ringing, beeping, buzzing, clinking, and clunking. I looked at it in disbelief. It drove me crazy. I made a quick trip back to the Verizon store to find out how to get the dumb thing –forget smart– under control.

Kids become indoctrinated into this noise thing at a very early age. When my daughters were little, they played with things like a hobby horse, baby drink and wet, a doll house, and not to be overly sexist I also bought them the Fisher Price parking garage. It came with a set of cars. You could send one up an elevator or careen another down a ramp. None of these toys had much in the way of noise unless you added your own: "Neigh!" as you galloped your horse or "Vroom-Vroom!" as you moved your car.

Today, though, almost all toys come with noise. They whirr, beep, whine, sing, play music, giggle, chortle, hum, honk, toot, buzz. Just take a walk down the toy aisle in Wal-Mart and you'll see what I mean. All this noise, coming at kids from the moment they are born!

Then, they grow up a little and enter the world of --- electronics --- and something devious happens. This is when noise goes underground – or at least under the skin. This is when noise becomes internalized and virtual worlds take control.

My three youngest grandchildren came to visit recently, minus parents. It was just the kids. At the airport I got a pass so I could meet them at the gate. Ages 12, 10, and 6, they came off the plane looking like typical kids – baseball caps on their heads, backpacks on their backs, wild fluorescent colored tennis shoes on their feet, an electronic something or other stuck to one hand, earphones dangling from the other. The three hour plane ride more or less depleted their batteries so one of the first things they wanted to know was where they could plug in.

Now my daughter is raising some great kids. They were polite, obedient, and they did listen – when their attention was not consumed by gadgets. When it was, I gave up because they were so engrossed in the virtual worlds inside their heads that they couldn't relate to the real world outside.

One of the things we did during their stay was to take the kids to Disneyworld. Gadgetry, for at least a while, was forgotten. They, like all the other kids we saw there, quickly became engrossed in the magic of the Magic Kingdom. It was refreshing. If the kids, however, were willing to let go of their virtual worlds, from what I saw, that was not true for many of the adults that were at the park. It was amazing! Everywhere I looked people (probably one in every three, and I'm not exaggerating) were glued to their phones. At Disneyworld! On the buses, on the rides, in the lines, at the restaurants, walking down Main Street! It was truly amazing. Eyes down, hands out in front, thumbs working away like mad! What were all these people doing? Were they sending an email? Reading a text message? Organizing pictures? I saw one lady playing Candy Crunch. Here they were at one of the premier vacation spots in the world; the sights, the sounds, the magic – all there in front of them. And where were these people? Stuck inside their heads, consumed by the virtual worlds inside their phones.

Outside noise and inside noise, so much for hearing. Now let's talk about the other thing our ears do. They listen. And this ability to listen sometimes runs in direct conflict to all the hearing that we do. It's only when the noise clears, only when it is quiet, only when it is still both outside and inside our heads; then, and only then, can we truly listen.

Listening. While hearing is a passive thing, listening is active. It requires you to engage and respond. Depending on your response, sometimes listening gives you the opportunity to become closer and closer to God. Let me show you what I mean.

Each of my daughters call me at least once a week. They are both busy women, juggling jobs, raising their kids – but when they call, we usually talk for about an hour. Actually, they talk. I listen. I hear about everything that is going right in their worlds and I hear about everything that is not. The calls often start with a sigh; but after an hour with Mom, they often end with a smile. All I have done is let them talk. A few well placed "uh huhs" and an occasional, pearly one-liner are all I need to say. This listening that I do becomes an act of love. It may even be wisdom, sometimes, depending on how pearly my one-liners are. Most definitely, though, listening to my daughters is an act of love.

Let me give you another example. I have a friend whom I have known since childhood. She is a woman with whom it is difficult to have a conversation. She loves to talk. When we visit, it is difficult for me to get a word in edgewise. My

111

occasional contribution to the dialog is quickly grabbed away so she can relate something else, usually something in which I have absolutely no interest. She effortlessly moves from one topic to another while I sit and – well, listen. Maybe you know someone like that. Maybe you are someone like that. Oops! My mother, with one of her pearly one-liners, once told me that if in conversation you talk all the time and don't stop to listen, you come away knowing only what you started with; and you never learn anything new. The "new" only comes if you stop to listen. So when I bear my friend's ramblings, I often think of my mother's words and I realize that while it might even be a little painful, I am the only one gaining. It puts a smile on my inner face, and I endure the visit. Listening, in this case, gives me a chance to practice my patience. Is it an act of love? Maybe. Nah, probably not, but it is definitely an act of patience.

One final example. My father was a story teller. He loved to relate accounts of things that happened to him as he was growing up. The problem was, he would relate them over and over again. I mentioned this before in a previous talk.

When I was younger, I groaned each time he started again on one of his favorite stories. As I grew older, though, I realized that while I was the listener, I was really not his intended audience. By my being there to listen, it gave him the chance to re-tell the stories to himself, which is all he really wanted to do; to relive his memorable adventures all over again. In the re-telling of his tales he was able to once again outwit his neighbor, get stuck in the mud and get himself out, win the prize, save his sister, escape the wrath of his mother. He could do all these things yet one more time and come out the hero all over again. When I understood that, being the listener became easy. It, too, became an act of love. Understanding is a gift of the Holy Spirit. Most assuredly, understanding was at play in me; but above all, it was an act of love.

Other pearly words of wisdom coming again from my mother were to be found in a poem on a little card that she kept attached by a magnet to the side of her refrigerator. When she died, I took the card to keep with my special things. It sums up what I am trying to say. It goes like this:

Prayer To Be A Better Listener

We don't really listen to each other, God. At least not all the time. Instead of true dialog, we carry on two parallel monologues. I talk. My companion talks. But what we are really concentrating on is how to sound good, how to make our points strongly, how to outshine the person we are talking with.

Teach us to listen as Your Son listened to everyone who spoke to Him. Remind us that, somehow, You are trying to reach us through our partner in conversation. Your truth, Your love, Your goodness are seeking us out in the truth, love, and goodness being communicated. When our words are harsh, hostile, or angry, we convey the very opposite of those qualities.

Teach us to be still, Lord, that we may truly hear our brothers and sisters, and in them, You. Amen.

You can grow closer to God just by being a good listener – for each other, yes, but also for God. He wants us to listen to Him. God? Talk to me? Are you serious? Me? Absolutely! All the time!

There is a song we sing in church. It's called "You Are Mine" and it was written by David Haas. Some of the lyrics are:

"I will come to you in the silence.

I will lift you up from all your fear.

You will hear My voice. I claim you as My choice.

Be still, and know I am near."

The things I liked most about my Emmaus retreat were the opportunities for quiet time. Maybe it was the same for you. My walks along the pathways, sitting by myself in the chapel, the quiet – all of the clutter removed from my brain. Why do we wait for a retreat experience to do that sort of thing – sit alone – be quiet – remove the clutter – be still?

I try, especially after Communion, to achieve that stillness. With a lot of other people in church sometimes that can be hard. Closing my eyes, sometimes, I find I can eliminate the noise from both outside and inside my head. With God inside me and my eyes closed I do feel His presence.

I have this philosophical discussion with myself every so often about this world and the next. I know God has some pretty wonderful things in store for me in the next world. I eagerly look forward to it. I also know that He has given me this world, with all its inherent noise, to find my way into the next.

When I sit quietly in church, especially right after Communion, I feel very close to God. And while one foot remains firmly planted in this world, a few toes of the other sometimes make their way into the next. It is a beautiful feeling.

Have you experienced it? It happens when you allow yourself the luxury of quiet. If you are missing out on that feeling, if you haven't heard God talking to you, I encourage you to try to find it. Make an effort to really calm your world. Then talk to God, directly. He listens in that calmness, in that quiet; and He will talk to you. No, you won't hear Him with your ears, but you will hear Him with your heart. Listen closely. You'll hear His "uh huhs"; and you'll hear His pearly one liners, too. He doesn't mind if you repeat yourself. He doesn't care if you ramble on and on. He is very patient. He listens. And He answers. It is His act of love.

Eyes

Ok, I've covered ears, nose, and even mouth. Now it's time to address our eyes. In preparing for this talk I took an informal poll. I asked several people: Of all the five senses of the human body, if you had to lose one, what one would you most hate to lose? The answer uniformly was sight. Those asked said they could tolerate losing their sense of smell, even taste. Hearing would be a rough one, but unquestionably, their sight would be the toughest one to lose.

The importance of sight makes perfect sense because our eyes are our windows to the world. They show, and help us to know, all that is around us – God's fabulously stunning creation. When you witness a sunset that spreads oranges and pinks, purples and reds across the sky; when you watch sun diamonds dance on an otherwise serene body of water; when you hold a newborn baby in your arms, don't you, as I do, thank God for all this beauty? Then I also thank Him for His gift of sight that allows me to enjoy it all.

This window, however, works two ways. We can see out, but at the same time, others can also look

117

in; which gives rise to what else our eyes have been called. They are also known as windows to our souls.

Many years ago, as a fledgling teacher, I took a class in storytelling. We learned technique and expression and all those good things that go into relating to a group of antsy children who would rather do anything but listen to you. This particular day, we met outside on the campus green. The teacher had invited some kids to the class so we could practice our newly learned skills. This was the early 70's and I vividly remember that I came dressed in my plaid bell bottom slacks and a crocheted vest, sporting the largest pair of Gloria Steinem sunglasses you could imagine. Was I cool or what? When it was my turn, I knelt down on the lawn in front of the kids and did my very best practiced rendition of an Aesop's Fable, *The Dog and His Bone*. Try as I might, the kids' attention began to wander. I didn't have them, and I knew it. I couldn't get them. And I didn't know why. I mean, I was actually your above average story teller, coasting through this class with an A in the bag. However, this time I could not connect with my audience. When I finished, I regrouped with my teacher and said, "Well, that was a bust." She laughed and then she said, "Do you know why?"

"No, why?" I asked.

"It's your sunglasses. The kids couldn't see your eyes." All of the expression coming through my mouth meant nothing because the kids could not see my eyes. Sure enough, I moved on to the next group, removed my Gloria Steinems, and had the kids hopping with laughter as I retold the exact same tale.

Eyes. What powerful organs! We can use them to express love – or hate, happiness – or sorrow, encouragement – or disgust, hope – or despair.

When my kids were growing up, I tried my best to stay out of their way when it came to making decisions. As long as their choices were not immoral or illegal, I tried to give them the freedom to soar or fall on their faces as the case may be. However, it was my eyes that deceived me. Once, my younger daughter announced a decision she had made that I did not particularly like. She looked at me, paused for a second, and then said, "What?"

"What do you mean - What?" I said.

"It's your look, Mother, that's what. You have that look. I can tell you don't agree with me."

Now I hadn't said a word, but I didn't have to. My eyes told the whole story.

Isn't that true for all of us? When we are happy, we put a smile on our face, but the twinkle? That's found in our eyes. When we are sad, our face may be gloomy, but it is our eyes that shed the tears.

Ok, so now, what do we do with those eyes? We see, right? And if we are all looking at the same thing, we should all be seeing the same thing, right? Wrong. The view from the top of the ladder is vastly different from the one at the bottom. (If you don't believe me, just ask any wife who has tried to wallpaper a room with her husband. It's not a pretty sight.)

Father Arthur, a retired priest at our parish, uses a technique quite often before he reads the gospel. He asks everyone in church to put themselves in the story he is about to tell; make themselves the leper being cleansed or the cripple being cured, or one of the crowd observing the miracle, or even make themselves Christ, Himself as He moves among the people. It's a great technique and helps those in church to look at the gospel and react to it in an entirely different way.

If ten people witness the same accident, the police expect there may be ten diverse descriptions of what occurred. What we see is tempered not only by our perspective but also by what we think, how we feel, and what experiences we have had before. These things are all wrapped up in something we call a point of view. Everyone has a different one.

Our point of view can make us sympathetic, antagonistic, inspire us to be patient, or make us ready to wring someone's neck. We interpret the things we see based on the principles and values we have developed or not developed for ourselves throughout our life. That's why we might see things one way when we are kids, a different way when we are 40, and an entirely different way when we are 60, 70, or even 80.

I had a funny exchange with this same daughter of mine, Ann, not too long ago. Today she is a rather meticulous housekeeper. When she was growing up, you needed a bulldozer to get through her room. She proceeded to give me an earful about her seventeen-year-old son who now could use that same bulldozer in his room; my grandson, who – while he does his own laundry – never puts the clean clothes away but rather retrieves them as needed from the bottom of his laundry basket. I came back with, "And you are looking for sympathy from me?" as I vividly remembered the same clean clothes depository sitting in the middle of her messy room. She went from enjoying her mess to being intolerant of her son's same kind of mess and will someday be like me, patient in the knowledge that the mess does eventually get replaced by an adulthood semblance of order. How it is seen is all in your point of view.

However, the eye I really want to talk about here is the mind's eye. That's the eye we use to see things, not exactly the way they are, but rather the way we would like them to be. When I look through my mind's eye I see myself, oh, say, 20 years younger and definitely 20 pounds lighter. Then I look in the mirror and what I would like is quickly replaced by the hard reality of what is.

We do all sorts of things with our mind's eye. We use it to dream our dreams, solve our problems, practice our upcoming challenging moments. Our mind's eye can even play little movies where we relive our accomplishments and, reluctantly, cringe at our regrets.

I use my mind's eye every morning as I lie in bed before I begin my day. I create my own little mental minder as I visualize what the day might bring. I picture myself in that meeting I know is scheduled, doing that ironing I know is piling up, calling the person who needs to hear from me. I actually do a dress rehearsal for my day, right inside my head. It's a handy little thing, that mind's eye.

However, unfortunately, I use it in other ways, too. The mind's eye is also where I safely store my prejudices, erect my walls, coddle my real or perceived slights. Grudges I hold are nursed in the eye of my mind because there I can suspend reality and see only what I want to see, hear only what I want to hear, and then I can justify it all to myself as I critique, criticize, and then (Oops!) judge. Hmmm! But I'm not the only one like this, I know.

A few years back a friend of mine came to visit and I brought her to mass with me. Though we were both raised in Catholic homes, went to Catholic schools, through some ancient misunderstanding she had been away from the church for some time and was there that day, with reservations, as a favor to me. As she saw the sacristans scurrying around, she leaned over to me and said, "They really think they're important, don't they?"

"Who?" I said.

"Those people setting everything up. They think they're holier than everyone else." I couldn't figure out what she meant by that. All I saw were hard-working, behind the scenes, church volunteers who generously gave of their time that day to make the mass run smoothly. What she saw was something else entirely. Her eyes were clouded by bitterness toward the church for who knows what long forgotten reason and the lenses she looked through were ones of antipathy and resentment.

There is a passage from the gospel of St. Luke that reads, "How can you say to your brother, 'Brother, let me take the speck out of your eye,' when you yourself fail to see the plank in your own eye?" That plank might be pride or jealousy or spite or one-up-manship. It might be hurt feelings or an ill-gotten grudge. Whatever it is, that plank is what keeps us from seeing things the way they really are and allows us to rely instead on the way we interpret them to be.

Those planks are what cause us to look at a clever, witty person and instead of admiring her witticism think, "Boy, get a load of her. What a show-off!" They are what get in our way when we see someone helping out or pitching in and, instead of being appreciative of her efforts, sniff at them and say, "She sure likes to run things, doesn't she?" Maybe we hear someone go overboard with compliments. On the outside we smile; but, because of those darn planks, on the inside we opine, "Good grief, what a brown nose!"

Take away all those planks, the mind's eye still has an inherent problem all its own. It has a very narrow perspective. It cannot see the bigger picture.

It can only see its own narrow slice. I had a very favorite principal when I was teaching. She gave me the freedom to be as creative as I wanted to be and rarely interfered with or objected to anything I wanted to do. However, one time she did say no to me. I don't even remember what it was about anymore, but I do remember her words. She said, "I see all sides here, Dot, and this is something we cannot do." And she was right. An excellent administrator, she considered the needs of everyone – the faculty, the students, the parents, and the district at large when making a decision. She saw the bigger picture in our school community where I could only see my own narrow slice.

And that's how it is with God. He is the all-seeing, all-knowing, ultimate administrator. We, from our narrow points of view, do not and cannot see it all – or know it all. We critique, criticize, and judge, without having access to the whole story. And that whole story? It's what is in the hearts of all those people we choose to judge.

Maybe someday, when we get to heaven, God will hold up that mirror that tells the truth. Just as I am not able to ignore those extra 20 years or those extra 20 pounds, there will be no pretending that things could be any other way than the way they really are. Our narrow slices of perception will dissolve because the big picture will be there for all to see, including what is in each and every heart.

But maybe, just maybe, there is a way to increase that narrow slice right now, even before we get to heaven. Once again I return to the Emmaus story in the gospel of St. Luke.

"When they neared the village to which they were going and Jesus acted as if he were going farther, they pressed Him, 'Stay with us. It is nearly evening. The day is practically over.' So He went in to stay with them. When He had seated Himself with them to eat, He took bread, pronounced the blessing, then broke the bread and began to distribute it to them. With that their eyes were opened...." Luke 24: 28-31.

This tells me the more we press God to stay with us, the more our eyes will be opened and the more of the picture we will be able to see. The closer we are to God the closer we come to understanding what is in the hearts of others. It happens when we sit down with Him to eat. It happens through the breaking of the bread. It happens through the Eucharist.

The great 14th century German theologian, Meister Eckhart, once said, "The eye through which I see God is the same eye through which God sees me." It goes both ways. Our window to the world is the window to our soul; and the window to our soul helps us find our place in the world.

We do have our work cut out for us though, removing those planks that sit in our eyes. And while we will never be able to see the entire picture while here on earth, we can work on increasing the size of our slice. We do it every time we sit down at the Table of the Lord to eat. May we all be blessed with a hearty, hunger-relieving, eye-opening appetite!

Growing Old Graciously

When I turned ten I wanted to be a cowboy. No, not a cowgirl, a cowboy! I watched Roy Rogers on television and I envisioned myself, not as Dale Evens, but as the big man himself. I wanted a cap gun for my birthday. I carried a leather zip-up wallet with boots engraved on one side and a horse's head on the other. I thought life would be complete, if I could only be a cowboy.

When I turned twenty, the cowboy dream was long abandoned in favor of loftier goals. I wanted to be a teacher; and I was well on my way to becoming one. Finish college, pick up that diploma and, without a doubt, life would be complete – when I became a teacher.

When I turned thirty, my teacher's hat was tucked away in favor of motherhood. My first daughter was born, my second on the way, and I spent my thirties as a full-time, stay-at-home mom. Baking brownies, wiping runny noses, reading bedtime stories – life couldn't get any better than that. Life was complete, now that I was a mother.

When I turned forty I realized that the brownies were just as good when bought at the store.

The runny noses could be managed competently by their individual owners. I still handled the bedtime stories but the siren's call of the classroom drew me back and I quickly found I could competently balance home and job with ease. Without a doubt, this was the pinnacle. Life could not get better than this.

Turning fifty gave me pause – but not for long. I was barraged by all the "over the hill" jokes that told me to greet middle age with a smile, or at least a smirk. So I went out and bought a sports car, a little merlot colored Miata with a stick shift and a convertible top that turned eyes as its now totally-in-charge-of-her-life owner drove by. Indeed, could life ever be better?

Sixty! I retired from the classroom once again, this time for keeps. I became an educational consultant and traveled the country giving talks, teaching seminars, sounding like the expert I was purported to be. People listened to me, looked up to me, and I said to myself, "How can it possibly get any better than this?"

Then one day, when I wasn't even looking, I turned seventy. How, in heaven's name I wondered, did that happen? With no major pitfalls, all body parts still functioning as they should, I had arrived at this milestone gracefully. Along the way, I learned a lot of lessons; some from my mother, others from my husband and my children, still others just from the rough and tumble seventy-plus years of living can bring. I had arrived gracefully, yes; but I'd like to think that through the lessons I learned, that I arrived graciously as well.

I learned that sometimes what I did not say was more important than what I said; that what I did not do was more important than all the things I did.

I learned when I talk too much and do not stop to listen, I never learn anything new.

I learned that paying someone a compliment or a concern costs me nothing. However, that same compliment or concern could be priceless to the one receiving it.

I learned not to worry about what others might say about me behind my back. If they were talking about me they were leaving someone else alone.

I learned I wasn't always right and to admit when I was wrong. That admission often made me more right than I thought I was in the first place.

I learned that "Let's agree to disagree" are powerful words. If both sides of any argument could agree on that alone, they have come to an agreement on something.

I learned to say "I'm sorry" and truly mean it.

I learned that some battles just can't be won and it is a waste of time trying to fight them.

I learned that some unwinnable battles can be won, if I ask God for help.

I learned that God wants to be asked.

Put them all together and they become my philosophy of life. They come as a result of years of living, from looking back at the many, many experiences life has sent my way. They were born out of successes I achieved and failures I endured. Today they define the way I live and determine the decisions I make. They make me into me.

My ten-year-old grandson was recently asked by his teacher to compose a bucket list. What goals did he want to set as his young life moved forward? His items included:

Score a winning goal from mid-field.

Go on a family trip.

Get a scholarship.

Get married.

Have a career.

Go to Germany.

Have a good life.

Die at 100.

Die happy.

What a list, I thought, keeping in mind that my life goal at ten was to be Roy Rogers! He, instead, touched on some universals. Aren't his wants the things we all want – a level of success (the winning mid-field goal), the closeness of family, financial stability, exciting adventures? Then, to finish it off with living to 100 and dying happy? Oh yes, count me in!

Looking forward, as one does with a bucket list, or looking backward, as one does with a list of life's lessons, both require some soul searching; both require some sorting out of what really is important. Both are exercises well worth taking on.

However, just as Roy Rogers gave way to loftier goals – career to motherhood, motherhood to career, either one to retirement; just as merlot Miatas will eventually give way to walkers and possibly wheelchairs; just as 50 and 60 eventually turned into 70, life continues to march on. My philosophy of life, my life's lessons and how well I learned them, determine how graciously I march along with it. I will continue to travel the Emmaus Road. I'm sure I will continue to stumble on it too. I may even have another life lesson in store for me because they come when you least expect them. They sneak up on you. And yes, they come in the darnedest of ways.

Coda

What is there that makes one life more special than any other? I read the biographies of movie stars or war heroes and presidents and I say to myself, "What makes reading about their lives any better or more important than reading about yours or mine?"

So it was with great arrogance that I assembled stories from my life to write these essays for you. I have taken you through many of my meaningful moments, times that jumped out of my memory and begged for attention. Each one strikes a chord in what remains my still unfinished symphony.

It is my hope that my stories have encouraged you to re-visit moments in your own life, to find meaning for yourself in what I had to say. Then your notes, along with mine, might produce some beautiful music together. And with God holding the conductor's baton, who knows what kind of masterful concert we might create! Surely we will bring to life the motto of the Emmaus sisterhood as we prove through each other, once again, that Jesus Christ is Risen! He is Risen Indeed!

About the Authors

Dot Minzer is a retired grandma who lives in Punta Gorda, Florida. A former teacher, media specialist, and educational consultant, Dot has been writing and sharing stories since she was eight years old. It all began in third grade when her class was asked to write an essay about the foreign missions. Her essay was good enough that she was asked to visit other classrooms and read her work to them. And in the doing, a love affair with the written word began.

Still a Project Junkie, Dot currently juggles several whirling plates. She is a hospital Eucharistic minister, serves as a lector at both daily and Sunday mass, volunteers with the St. Vincent DePaul Society, is co-facilitator for her parish Emmaus Retreat Ministry, and, along with her husband Ed, is an avid sailor. They have taken Classy Lady, their Catalina 387 sailboat, throughout Florida waters and to the Bahamas many times.

The Holy Spirit is a master story teller. He resides everywhere and anywhere, in every heart that welcomes Him and also those that don't. His ideas greatly enhance those of any writer asking for His help.

Made in the USA
San Bernardino, CA
22 June 2016